I0529017

Jesus and Mental Health

1st Century vs *21st Century*

Marvin K. Lucas
Evangelist and Licenced Counselor
MEd, MAR, LPC

Foreword by Jason D. Kushner PhD

ILLUMINATION
PUBLISHERS

Jesus and Mental Health. 1st Century vs 21st Century
©2022, Marvin Lucas

All rights are reserved. No part of this book may be duplicated, copied, translated, reproduced or stored mechanically, digitally, or electronically without specific, written permission of the author and publisher. Author photograph by Mona Alviedo.

Unless otherwise indicated, all Scripture references are from the Holy Bible, New International Version®, NIV® Copyright ©1973, 1978, 1984, 2011 by Biblica, Inc.® Used by permission. All rights reserved worldwide.

ISBN: 978-1-953623-87-4. Printed in the United States.
Cover Design by Roy Appalsamy of Toronto, Canada.

About the Author: Marvin contributes his unique perspective, experiences, and education to this book. Marvin has two master's degrees, one in general counseling and one in pastoral counseling. He has had his own counseling practice for several years specializing in couples counseling and anxiety, stress, and anger management. For the last four years, Marvin has been a professor of counseling at the University of Arkansas in Little Rock. He grew up as an atheist in the United Kingdom and became a Christian in his mid-twenties. Marvin has done missions and ministry in the USA, Europe, and Asia. He has been married for over thirty years and has two children in their twenties. His other works are *Baguette Moments* and *Capes and Tiaras,* which can be purchased at ipibooks.com. Marvin can be contacted at marvin@mklcounseling.com. His website is mklcounseling.com.

ILLUMINATION PUBLISHERS   www.ipibooks.com

Acknowledgments

I want to thank my wife for her love and for helping me with my mental health through our thirty-plus years of a wonderful marriage. In addition, I appreciate Norman Davis' and Kevin Herman's long-term friendships and emotional and spiritual support. Thanks to Dr. Jason Kushner for being a friend and mentor in my counseling career and professorship.

_____ Contents _____

PART I – JESUS AND MENTAL HEALTH

_____ Contents _____

Foreword

I have had the privilege of witnessing Marvin in his role as a minister and as a teacher of counseling to religious and nonreligious audiences alike, and in those capacities, he weaves a tapestry of helping whose broad audiences find comfort in and strength from the best elements offered by the Scriptures and counseling practices. Readers of this book will understand the various ways that humans find help from each other, social creatures that we are, and the ways that passages from the Bible explain so much about the human condition with which we are all familiar. Within a framework of comfort and familiarity, Marvin takes readers on a journey that addresses a comprehensive list of modern psychological stressors such as, but not limited to, depression, anxiety, social phobia, self-harm, mood disorders, and his unique take on spiritual abuse while also including spiritual insights, therapist notes, and self-care tips. Marvin narrates his compelling life story and testimony to witness the transformative power of faith.

An ordained pastor and licensed professional counselor with master's degrees in divinity and counseling, Marvin crafted this book, *Jesus and Mental Health?*, from the perspective of bridging the secular and spiritual worlds into a sensible, easy-to-follow guide for those on a path toward self-help for common psychological concerns and maladies with tools common to secular counseling, along with specific and relevant passages of the New Testament with a focus on understanding the self better through the words of the Bible and the life of Jesus.

> —Dr. Jason D. Kushner PhD
> Director of the Counselor
> Education program at the
> University of Arkansas at
> Little Rock

Introduction

> The church across North America has struggled to minister effectively with children, teens, and adults with common mental health conditions and their families. One reason for the lack of ministry is the absence of a widely accepted model for mental health outreach and inclusion.
>
> —Stephen Grcevich MD

Why has the church "struggled" with the acceptance of mental health? Can mental health and the church coexist? Will one be compromising their faith if they seek therapy? According to Dr. Ed Stetzer, many suffer in the church because of the "shame and stigma" that can be attached to seeking mental health services. This book will examine the science and the Bible (Jesus) to see if these two beliefs can coexist.

What is the perception of mental health in the church?

- 27 percent of churches have a plan to assist families affected by mental illness.

- 53 percent of churchgoers with mental illness say the church has been supportive.

- 76 percent of churchgoers say suicide is a problem that needs to be addressed in their community.

- 4 percent of churchgoers who have lost a loved one

to suicide say church leaders were aware of their loved one's struggles.

- 35 percent of Americans say mental illness could be overcome with Bible study and prayer alone.

—Lifeway Research 2018

These stats validate Dr. Grcevich's belief that the church is struggling to be open about worries, doubts, and fears. Many believe that the church is not a compassionate place for airing mental health issues like anxiety, depression, and stress. Many use simple statements like "Pray," "Read your Bible," "Just repent," or "You have no faith" in an attempt to pacify the person. Unfortunately, these harsh statements can push congregants to hide their mental health issues.

When one looks at the research, it shows that people are afraid to let others know about their sins, temptations, struggles, and doubts, and so put on a smiley face for church services and Bible studies. Since everybody is doing this, nobody realizes that everybody is afraid that others will discover who they really are and feel guilty that they seem to deal with issues and temptations that nobody else faces. Fear and shame keep us from being honest and opening up to others about our struggles.

—redeeminggod.com

Because of all these factors, the church can be a breeding ground for mental health issues because of its culture where no one is seen to struggle and no one confesses sins. In contrast, the world has embraced caring for mental health; this is shown by a 2018 Barna survey, which stated that 78 percent of society have either gone to or are entirely open to counseling, but the church is way behind in accepting counseling. Even Jesus describes us as being "harassed and helpless," a mental health statement if I have ever heard one! We are helpless but somehow not seeking help!

However, can we find mental health advocates in the pulpit? Here are the stats:

- 49 percent of pastors say they rarely or never speak to their congregation about mental illness.

- 23 percent of pastors acknowledge they have personally struggled with a mental illness.

—Lifeway Research

Considering this research, leaders are not immune to having mental health issues. Here is an interesting fact: Some of the most outstanding pastors, theologians, and founders of churches like C.S. Lewis, Charles Spurgeon, Mother Theresa, and Martin Luther, among many others, struggled with depression and a host of other mental health disorders (crosswalk.com). The late Jarrid Wilson, who was a megachurch leader, had several severe episodes of depression and did not tell anyone about his inner torment. His pain became unbearable; he found himself sitting alone in a hotel room with a gun on his lap! He was able to seek help and become an advocate for mental health. He said about the church culture that churches present an image of perfection/performance, but "churches should look more like psych wards."

The ultimate question is, did Jesus have mental health struggles? Yes, many times. Jesus struggled with a mental health crisis in the Garden of Gethsemane, where he stated that he was "overwhelmed to the point of death." However, Jesus was able to fight for faith when his mind was saying no. Jesus showed and expressed all his emotions, not hiding his fear, pain, joy, love, or suffering. Sadly, this expression of emotion, this openness, can be the opposite in church culture. Jesus could handle his life stressors and have emotional reserves available to help others. I want to end this introduction with a compassionate quote from Jesus:

> *"Take my yoke upon you and learn from me, for I am gentle and humble in heart, and you will find rest for your souls."* (Matthew 11:29)

Many will pick up this book looking for understanding, clarity, or closure. I wish I could say that with my two master's degrees, one in Bible pastoral counseling and one in secular counseling, I will be able to answer all your questions, but you might leave frustrated or a little angry. For centuries, many scholars like Socrates, Plato, Gestalt, Adler, and Freud have tried to tackle the labyrinth of the mind and have come up short. One thing I do know is that Jesus is "gentle and humble" and far more compassionate than I am. I am aware of my limitations in this vast topic, but my prayer and hope are that God will lead you to a greater peace of mind while helping you "find rest for your soul."

I am excited to embark on this journey to bridge the church and mental health gap. One goal I hope to achieve is to show that Jesus has extraordinary sensitivity to those with depression, grief, anxiety, and stress. Although Jesus is known as the "Wonderful Counselor," I am a licensed counselor, which pales in comparison, so when Jesus states, "Learn from me," I am humbled. I have a lot to learn, and hopefully you will pick up something new along the way!

Mental Health Caution

When it comes to depression, anger, anxiety, phobias, and grief, there can be many reasons and levels of severity. This book will try to help people with mild to moderate conditions. It focuses on brief solution counseling; it is not for those who need extensive therapy for acute trauma like sexual abuse, domestic abuse, childhood trauma, molestation, rape, PTSD, etc. For such people, this book could be detrimental to your mental health, and I advise you not to read it. If you suffer from these traumas, see a qualified counselor immediately for your own personalized care.

Part I

Jesus and Mental Health

Chapter 1

Jesus and Depression

Signs of Depression

- Persistent sadness, anxiety, or "empty" mood
- Feelings of hopelessness or pessimism
- Irritability
- Feelings of guilt, worthlessness, or helplessness
- Loss of interest or pleasure in hobbies and activities
- Decreased energy or fatigue
- Moving or talking more slowly
- Feeling restless or having trouble sitting still
- Difficulty concentrating, remembering, or making decisions
- Difficulty sleeping, early-morning awakening, or oversleeping
- Appetite and/or weight changes
- Thoughts of death or suicide, or suicide attempts
- Aches or pains, headaches, cramps, or digestive problems without a clear physical cause and/or that do not ease even with treatment

—CDC

One does not have to have all these symptoms to be depressed and diagnosed with a disorder, and one must have them for at least two weeks.

The first interaction we will look at is Jesus with the bleeding woman. This woman had been bleeding for twelve years and had gone to many so-called specialists, but unfortunately, many of these would have had barbaric practices, and sadly, her health went from bad to worse. After every botched operation or quack potion, her sense of hopelessness deepened. This ailment had been with her for years. Persistent bleeding can leave one weak and with low energy. Also, according to Jewish law, she was considered unclean because of her bleeding. This label meant she could not have close contact with others, including touch. Put yourself in her shoes and consider that she could not be physically consoled or comforted in a time when she needed it the most. Her own family could not even touch her! Because of her prolonged depression due to her health, today, if she went to a psychiatrist, she would probably be diagnosed with persistent depressive disorder (also called dysthymia) that lasts for at least two years. Her prognosis and her profound sense of hopelessness made her a high risk for one who might consider suicide.

When I read Scripture or talk to someone with chronic pain, I try to put myself in their emotional and mental space, then look at my life experiences to connect with their pain. I have to really listen and empty myself to take in their experience of pain. I do not struggle with depression, but recently I have been having severe back pain. Pain killers, TENS electro treatment, chiropractic visits, and acupuncture to relax my muscles didn't work. My chronic pain went on for months, affecting my sleep and overall mood. Some days I wondered if my pain would ever end. I wouldn't verbally share my experience with a woman bleeding for twelve years, but it helps me have an empathic connection.

This woman had heard of a teacher healing the sick; the blind were seeing, and the paralyzed were walking. Is this true? What kind of witchcraft is this? Is this guy real or a myth? She had chased false hopes before. Just imagine you are in this woman's predicament and totally out of options, and you hear stories of this miracle worker who could heal you. The bleeding limits her mobility. She is exhausted mentally and physically, but she sets out for her miracle.

On the journey, she must have envisioned Jesus coming up to her and touching her, saying some compassionate words, and she would get her strength back. The woman finally arrives, drained and dehydrated from loss of blood and from her journey, and to add to her plight, she could see Jesus, but a crowd surrounded him. The Scriptures state that he was literally pressed by the crowd. How is she going to get her healing? She attempted to approach Jesus, but she was hesitant because of her unclean condition and genuine fear of being banished. Her idea was to go down to her knees and touch the hem of his cloak. She might have been so exhausted that all she could do was crawl to Jesus. She might have gotten on her knees, got as close as she could, and lunged out, grabbing the edge of his cloak. To her amazement, life came back into her body, and she could stand. Awed and frightened, she walked away, trying to take in all these feelings that she had not felt in twelve years. She was probably crying in fear, confusion, and joy. Then she heard, "Who touched me?" The crowd was confused because there were so many around him. Jesus looked around and saw one person walking away when everyone else was pressed against him, a person who looked like they had stolen something they did not ask for. Sheer horror and guilt must have seized her. Should she run? Should she go back? Was he going to take back her healing?

Her choice was to face her fear and plead on her knees to Jesus. Jesus looked at her with loving compassion and listened to her suffering. He told her, "Go in peace." If she had left without this intervention, she would have left with guilt and dread, wondering if one day his disciples would track her down and take back her blessing. Jesus wanted the bleeding to stop, but she would have left bleeding with guilt and shame (a depressive condition). Her body was healed, but her conscience was unclean. How many of us have been healed in Christ but then take on shame and guilt that God wants us to be free of? If we have a "glass half empty" attitude, we are constantly looking for something to add to our own cognitive label of "failure," "cursed," "loser," or "thief," but Jesus does not see us this way.

One of the goals of this book is to take the mystery out of mental health. Jesus and the bleeding woman's interaction was short. Jesus used brief cognitive behavior therapy (CBT) to focus specifically on a "person's train of thought and identify problematic patterns of negative thinking. These thinking patterns stimulate negative thoughts and interpretations of the patient's self and their world" (betterhelp.com). The bleeding woman's actions were not the best by stealing a miracle, but Jesus forgave her, and he wanted to make sure she was not guilt-ridden. We see in this interaction that Jesus is passionate about us living a guilt-free life. Jesus is concerned about our emotional and mental health. So go in peace!

Spiritual Insight

Go to Jesus first before looking for humanistic answers. Do not go to him last. It could save you much pain. You may experience obstacles (a crowd) to get your healing.

Personal Narrative

Depression is something my wife has been dealing with for twenty-plus years, and as a husband, I get a front-row seat to her pain and suffering. Some days it has been so bad that she cannot get out of bed. On her more challenging days, I try to listen to her, support her, and pray with her. She is a resilient woman and my hero.

Therapist Note

Long-term circumstances such as an oppressive relationship, a chronic health condition, a dead-end job, an abusive boss, partner, or friend, or a sick loved one, can bring on a sense of hopelessness that can lead to clinical depression, which depletes happy chemicals like serotonin in your brain.

Quick Self-Care Tip

Create your own happy chemicals. I know you do not feel like it! However, get up and get out. Watch a funny movie, sing your favorite worship song, hang out with a FUN friend! Fun and being social creates endorphins, dopamine, oxytocin, and serotonin (happy chemicals).

Resource for Depression

Healthline.com, "6 Ways to Boost Serotonin without Medication."

Also see Chapter 14 for free resources, strategies, and helplines.

Chapter 2

Jesus and Cyclothymic Disorder

(Mild to Moderate Mood Swings)

Hypomanic Symptoms

- An exaggerated feeling of happiness or well-being (euphoria)
- Extreme optimism
- Inflated self-esteem
- Talking more than usual
- Racing thoughts
- Irritable or agitated behavior
- Excessive physical activity
- Increased drive to perform or achieve goals (sexual, work related, or social)

Depressive Symptoms

- Feeling sad, hopeless, or empty
- Tearfulness
- Irritability, especially in children and teenagers
- Loss of interest in activities once considered enjoyable
- Changes in weight
- Feelings of worthlessness or guilt
- Thinking of death or suicide

In the Bible we see countless interactions with Jesus, most approached with absolute reverence and humility. Here are some of them: "Lord, have mercy on me," "I am not worthy," and "Have pity on us." One individual came to Jesus with an audacious question: "What shall I do to get to heaven?" I think that is a great question, but I would have to be doing well spiritually, attending church, giving tithes, having no unconfessed sin, and feeling super confident to approach Jesus with it. The rich young ruler approached Jesus in this way. He enthusiastically confirmed that he hadn't committed adultery, and never stole, lied, or disrespected his parents. Wow! What a moral resumé. Outside of adultery, I broke all these by the time I was sixteen! The man was expecting Jesus to say, "Collect $200 and go straight to heaven." But Jesus responded with love because he wanted the man to excel spiritually and emotionally: "You lack one thing: go and sell all you have and give to the poor." The young man could have responded by saying, "Can you help me?" or "I am working on this," but the passage says these words devastated him. How can a person go from total confidence to devastation? Without saying another word, he walked away from Jesus, dejected.

What happened here? How can an individual have extreme mood swings in seconds? This man was vocal about his strengths but hid his shortcomings.

> Ignoring a problem does not make it go away. In fact, it can simmer away beneath the surface and lead to poor mood and energy levels, and can also cause your moods to become unstable.   –Liz Miller

When one is emotionally unstable, it is easy to fall apart when someone questions or challenges their character or worldview. Not acknowledging and working on our weaknesses makes us hypersensitive to criticism and even to helpful truth and instruction. Sometimes we cannot tell the difference, and we just run away, or we attack or gossip about that person. Jesus, full of compassion and love, can override irrational insecurities and impulsive fears. A person who is never growing emotionally is hard to be around. They seem to play the relationship yo-yo game of I love you today/hate you tomorrow/love you the next day. Being around such a person can create extreme insecurities, and a false self-image can also be created. Self-image is personified through the social media craze that is addictive to this generation, with selfies, personal YouTube channels, and personal blogs. We see vicious attacks on people with differing opinions, especially regarding politics, gender views, and religion. Some individuals are not seeking to understand, but are using extreme labels like racist, bigot, and homophobic to shut down conversations surrounding these topics (see Chapter 8).

There is a dark side to this disorder. We are sometimes surprised to hear that a person is happy one day and tries to take their life the next day. I grew up in the UK, where the most popular sport is soccer. A charismatic player named Gary Speed took his life at forty-two years of age. Here's what a friend said about him:

> Speaking on BBC News today, former Wales teammate Robbie Savage said: "I just can't believe it. He was my mate and he's gone. I've got very close to Gary in the last few years—the guy is a trooper, he's

left two gorgeous kids behind and a beautiful wife. He had everything; he had everything. I spoke to him yesterday and we were laughing and joking.... That's what Gary's like—he always thinks about other people."

As a therapist, the people who concern me are those who are happy all the time and those who are sad all the time. What is unfortunate is that the ones who are always happy can be deceiving. We all have weaknesses and challenges; when we don't acknowledge them, we deceive ourselves and are open to extreme insecurities.

Paul Hudson did an article on "9 Things Insecure People Do That Ruin Their Lives."

> The more insecure you are, the more that insecurity weighs on your mind. You think more about it and think less about anything else. You live in fear, hoping that no one notices how flawed you are, even if only in one regard.
>
> You're scared of interacting with people because you don't want them to see through you. People judge...that's the way that we're built. The real question is: Why does it matter to you so much? Most people won't be as upset with your flaw as you imagine, to begin with. —elitedaily.com

What do you do when you are confronted? Do you flee, freeze, or fight? The soccer player in this story took flight.

I have been married for thirty years, and though I know my wife loves me, I can still get uncomfortable when I'm challenged by her or faced with my weakness. My initial reaction is to get defensive or deflect. Here are some things that help us when these moments arise:

> The first step is to allow yourself to be aware of, experience, and move through the full range of your feelings, both pleasant and unpleasant.... In this case, it means dealing with eight unpleasant feelings: sadness, shame, helplessness, anger, vulnerability, embarrassment, disappointment, and frustration. Allowing yourself to move toward pain and deal with the feelings that result from disappointment, builds emotional strength. —Psychology Today

We will never change if we constantly give in to these unpleasant moments. Stay and say, "No! I'm not going to run, fight, or make excuses." You will surprise yourself and others around you. Having faith and trusting God in these moments is one step closer to heaven.

Spiritual Insight

What are your thoughts about this scripture? "I will boast all the more gladly about my weaknesses, so that Christ's power may rest on me. That is why, for Christ's sake, I delight in weaknesses, in insults, in hardships, in persecutions, in difficulties. For when I am weak, then I am strong" (2 Corinthians 12:9–10). Do you have a balanced conversation with others expressing the good and the not-so-good? The rich young ruler did not boast in his weaknesses but his strengths (more on this in Chapter 12).

Personal Narrative

I grew up in Section 8 housing, and I had to hustle and fight for everything. When I was confronted, I got angry and physically hurt people. Over the years I have learned how to focus on my weaknesses such as my pride and anger, and on forgiveness and being honest with myself. I have learned to control my destructive impulses and now enjoy it when people are brutally honest with me. I prefer that to hidden attitudes.

Therapist Note

If you think of the people that get under your skin, they are predictable. You know that Dad, brother, coworker, the boss will be their annoying selves today, but you act surprised every time. You respond to the triggers. Jesus always speaks the loving truth, so why was the rich young man surprised that he fell short, since we all do? People are predictable, so prepare yourself for that disappointed look, the negative comment, the sarcasm, and ride it out. Don't give in to your primitive impulses; rise above them, and show people your new emotional maturity.

Quick Self-Care Tip

When you are emotionally up to it, attempt to be honest with yourself. Write down your weaknesses and embrace them, and your emotional floor will be closer to your ceiling. Then try to bring a small weakness of yours into general conversation with others and see the power in weakness.

Paul Hudson wrote:

The fact is that you're awesome. You're not perfect, but no one is. The only thing you should be insecure about is being irrational—everything else is subjective and out of your control. By being insecure, you tell yourself that you're not good enough the way you are. That's a lie.   —elitedaily.com

Chapter 3

Jesus and Anxiety Disorder

Signs of High-Functioning Anxiety

On the Outside

- Hardworking
- Detail oriented
- High achieving
- Ambitious
- Perfectionist
- Organized
- Well prepared
- Calm
- Does well under pressure

On the Inside

- Overthinking
- Overwhelmed
- Burned out
- Has trouble saying no
- Needs to be busy
- Has unrealistic expectations
- People pleaser
- Fears failure
- Full of self-doubt
  –becalmwithtati.com

There's tension in the house. Two sisters are preparing for a special guest; the older one is rushing around, and the other is helping at a slower pace. The older one is washing a glass vigorously and constantly holding it up to the light to see if it is sparkling clean. "I just washed that," protests Mary, shaking her head. "But I saw a water mark on it," insists Martha. Martha looks around and, stressed, says, "Everything has to be perfect tonight, and did you clean the dust on top of the window?" "Yes," replies Mary. Martha continues, "Good, don't forget to clean under the rug too." "Isn't that a bit much?" questions Mary. "No, he could trip on the carpet and see the dirt under there too," contends Martha. Then Mary is saved by a knock at the door. Martha rushes to the door and barely greets their guest because she must finish cooking. Jesus comes in and sits in the living area, and Mary follows him. She is excited to have the Teacher in their home and has prepared several questions for him. Martha is in the kitchen, deliberately clanging pots loudly. She occasionally peers into the living area, hoping to catch Mary's attention to help, but after ten minutes, it is too much. Finally, Martha is at a boiling point. She storms into the living room and shouts, "Jesus, tell her to help me!"

Jesus shows her compassion by saying, "Martha, Martha, you are anxious and troubled about many things, and Mary has chosen the right one" (ESV). This wasn't the only time she was anxious; it was a way of life for her, and Jesus called her out. Even if she sat down, her mind would be racing, and she could not focus on the opportunity of a lifetime.

My heart goes out to Martha; she is tormented by perfectionism and unhealthy expectations. Martha is like many of us who struggle with anxiety—we are so busy that we miss the special moments in our lives. We can even serve at church with high anxiety when we should be serving the Prince of Peace! Unfortunately, Martha majored in minors, living a high-activity life with little emotional reward.

Thich Nhat Hanh writes:

We have negative mental habits that come up over and over again. One of the most significant negative habits we should be aware of is constantly allowing our minds to run off into the future. Perhaps we got this from our parents. Carried away by our worries, we're unable to live fully and happily in the present. Deep down, we believe we can't really be happy just yet—that we still have a few more boxes to be checked off before we can really enjoy life. So we speculate, dream, strategize, and plan for these "conditions of happiness" that we want to have in the future, and we continually chase after that future, even while we sleep. We may have fears about the future because we don't know how it's going to turn out, and these worries and anxieties keep us from enjoying being here now.

If our anxiety is constant, it can affect our quality of life by giving us poor sleep, digestion issues, headaches, migraines, high blood pressure, racing heart, and in severe cases, panic attacks. The Anxiety and Depression Association of America warns us:

> People with an anxiety disorder are three to five times more likely to go to the doctor and six times more likely to be hospitalized for psychiatric disorders than those who do not suffer from anxiety disorders.
> –adda.org

Our physical and mental health are severely compromised with prolonged high anxiety. We all live with a certain level of anxiety to keep us responsible and conscientious. Keeping anxiety low and efficiency up is a delicate balance in life. In corporate America, in colleges and schools (especially during finals), we are under the false impression that we are not working hard enough if we are not stressed. If you are joyful at work, you are a slacker! There is a point when anxiety or stress become counterproductive. Here are some stats to consider:

> Stress and worry can reduce an individual's productivity by up to 77%. This dip in productivity is partly because over 20 percent of workers spend more than five hours on the clock each week thinking about their stressors and worries.
>
> –American Institute of Stress 2020

Martha's anxiety could have made her preparations longer; instead, she could have been present or relaxed when Jesus arrived. Unfortunately, anxiety can be very deceptive—somehow, we feel that we will finally find the end of the industrious rainbow through our busyness, but the hunger of anxiety never seems satisfied, leaving us full of self-doubt, overwhelmed, and with a sense of being perpetually stressed.

Jesus knew how this cognition could hinder our relationship with his Father, and he was an advocate for a worry-free life. There's no greater expression of this conviction than in the Sermon on the Mount. Jesus addressed many things, such as fellowship, forgiveness, and the poor, and he made clear his thoughts about anxiety as well.

Jesus' first words on this topic are, "Therefore I tell you, do not worry about your life." Wow, Jesus, can't I have a little worry? You don't have my life, kids, job, spouse, or childhood. Jesus understood how worry could undermine a relationship with God. What is worry? It's fear. Fear is the opposite of faith. He also rebukes those with this mindset, stating, "You of little faith." Jesus is not going to negotiate with our excuses to fret.

I would like to remind us of Jesus' words, adding some emphasis of my own: "Martha, "Martha, you are anxious and troubled about many THINGS." In Jesus' sermon on worry, he states, "For the pagans run after all these THINGS." Pagans run after things. What is a pagan? Having grown up in England, I am familiar with paganism. Pagan worship is polytheism, which means many gods, the opposite of being a Christian, a believer. Would any of us say, "I'm an unbeliever"? No, I'm on the worship team, I put the donation drives together, or I am a deacon! We consider unbelievers to be immoral, drunkards, and liars. How about anxious people? When we are anxious and not trusting in God, we are the same as the immoral person. Anxiety/fear is the opposite of faith/trust. We must see the seriousness of our anxiety. Jesus is not going to negotiate our faithlessness in our circumstances.

Jesus continues his thoughts on worry: "But seek first his kingdom and his righteousness, and all these THINGS will be given to you as well." Mary decided to do the right thing; she sought after Jesus' teaching. Mary was rewarded, while Martha felt empty and exasperated. Jesus concludes his teaching on anxiety with, "Therefore do not worry about tomorrow, for tomorrow will worry about itself." He encourages us to live in the now, not tomorrow. However, don't be surprised that every day there are troubles, so we must learn to manage our anxiety.

Therapy Note

Write out a priority list and consider the THINGS that really matter. You will have to find a new conviction to keep these priorities. You can't put cleaning or business in front of Jesus. You have to be happy with a few dirty dishes or business calls and emails that can wait until tomorrow. This will take discipline, but you will see that life or business will not implode without every moment of your attention!

Quick Self-Care Tip

Anxious people put unsaid expectations on themselves above and beyond their job description. Decide to stop the spin cycle. First, take all your lunch breaks outside the office. Next, do not bring your work home, and you might have to say no to additional work. Also, most anxious people do not take their full allotment of vacation days, so take them and go somewhere you can relax. Mothers, get your older kids doing chores and take a "mommy free day" having someone you trust take care of the kids for a few hours. A few hours or a few days will help. (See other self-care tips in the mindfulness chapter.)

Scripture Challenge

Read this scripture five times: "The mind governed by the flesh is death, but the mind governed by the Spirit is life and peace. The mind governed by the flesh is hostile to God; it does not submit to God's law, nor can it do so. Therefore, those who are in the realm of the flesh cannot please God" (Romans 8:6–8). Get your life back! God has equipped us with the Holy Spirit, the same power that raised Jesus from the dead, so that we can have a victory over our anxiety. Decide to have peace and not unbelief.

Personal Narrative

My son, who is in his mid-twenties, has been diagnosed with high anxiety; in the last year, he has had several panic attacks. The pain of my son suffering was heart-wrenching for me as a father. I felt helpless watching him in tears, trapped by anxiety. He needed to reset, to make some major lifestyle and spiritual changes. Today he is the happiest he has been in years, and his anxiety stays low.

Resource
Setting boundaries at work: https://psychcentral.com/blog/tips-for-setting-boundaries-at-work

Chapter 4

Jesus and Social Fears

Psychological

- Avoiding social situations
- Extreme and irrational anxiety
- Severe fear of judgment and rejection
- Intense feelings of self-consciousness
- Wanting to talk to others but experiencing much difficulty and fear

Physical

- Blushing
- Sweating
- Trembling
- Nausea
- A rapid heart rate
- Rigid body posture, making little eye contact, or speaking with an overly soft voice

The pandemic has heightened our social fears. For those who have lived through it, our social habits have permanently changed. My social spacing has increased, and my anxiety increases when I'm around crowds, especially indoors. So it is not surprising that those contacting the distress hotline went up by 1000 percent (SAMSA).

A person who had their own social anxiety is the Samaritan woman Jesus met at Jacob's well. Unfortunately, many of her social fears were based on her life choices and the cultural stigmas of the time. It is vital as a therapist to try to understand the genesis of a person's anxiety. Sometimes it comes from their childhood or decisions as an adult. Prolonged circumstances or poor choices can lead to a clinical diagnosis. This woman had several broken relationships and became a pariah in the village, which was why she went to the well at the hottest time of the day. She deliberately did this to avoid the crowds and the gossip during the cooler times of the day. Her life choices were one social barrier, and the other was being a Samaritan (a "half-breed" to the Jews). This hatred had been escalating for 600 years, as the Samaritans went to war in 108 BC and joined the Seleucids in attacking the Jews. The Jews retaliated by destroying their worship temple near Jacob's well. They had no place to worship in their day and were excluded from the temple in Jerusalem. A Jew did not associate with a Samaritan, let alone a woman, in the case of a man. This brings us to another issue, that of being a woman at that time and being treated as a second-class citizen. Here is a law that depicts the sentiment of the day:

> *The teachers of the law and the Pharisees brought in a woman caught in adultery. They made her stand before the group and said to Jesus, "Teacher, this woman was caught in the act of adultery. In the Law Moses commanded us to stone such women." (John 8:3–5)*

The punishment for adultery was to be stoned to death! But where was the adulterous man? Who was going to give this woman a fair hearing? This gender-biased mob had condemned the woman. In the first century, women did not have a voice. Even though Jesus stood up to the crowd and saved her life, this prejudice was prevalent at that time.

The Samaritan woman had many reasons to avoid society with her questionable past with men. A typical day in Israel is a hot one, and she hiked a mile and a half from her village of Sychar to get water from Jacob's well. Usually, there was no one there at the well at that time of day. Who else would willingly come out in that kind of extreme heat? As she approached the well, to her horror, a Jew was there. I imagine that her anxiety increased. She had been taught that she must avoid eye contact in these circumstances. This was the last thing she needed; all she wanted to do was simply fill her jar with water. He could spit on her, beat her, break her water jar or, at best, not even talk to her! She took a deep breath and made it to the well. Then, her worst fear—he spoke to her, "Will you give me a drink?" This is a trap, she thought. She reminded him, "You are a Jew and I am a Samaritan woman. How can you ask me for a drink?" Then the conversation turned weird. Jesus said, "If you knew the gift of God and who it is that asks you for a drink, you would have asked him and he would have given you living water." The woman thought this person must be full of himself saying "the gift of God"; and what is this living water? Still puzzled by what Jesus said, she responds. "Sir," the woman said, "you have nothing to draw with, and the well is deep. Where can you get this living water?" The conversation continues:

Jesus answered, "Everyone who drinks this water will be thirsty again, but whoever drinks the water I give them will never thirst. Indeed, the water I give them will become in them a spring of water welling up to eternal life."

The woman said to him, "Sir, give me this water so that I won't get thirsty and have to keep coming here to draw water."

He told her, "Go, call your husband and come back."

"I have no husband," she replied.

Jesus said to her, "You are right when you say you have no husband. The fact is, you have had five husbands, and the man you now have is not your husband. What you have just said is quite true.

"Sir," the woman said, "I can see that you are a prophet." (John 4:13–19)

Five husbands! One could possibly blame the other party for the first divorce or two. However, after a while, that individual becomes the common denominator. Then the conversation with Jesus turns deep, and the woman is faced with her actions and the consequences of her choices. Jesus used reality therapy here, which holds clients responsible for their behavior rather than blaming their environment, parents, or culture (R. E. Wubbolding, "Reality therapy and self-evaluation: The key to client change"). Here are more details:

Responsibility

A hyper-responsible person tries to act in a way that creates feelings of self-worth and worth to those around them. When unsuccessful at fulfilling their own needs, they deny the reality of the environment. They only become successful when they face that reality and fulfill their needs within that framework.

Right and Wrong

> Being worthwhile requires clients to maintain a reasonable standard of behavior, correcting themselves when they behave poorly and crediting themselves when they do things right.
>
> —William Glasser 2010

Jesus used this strategy long before William Glasser coined the phrase in the 1960s. Nobody had spoken to her like this, and she was amazed by how Jesus understood her. She was faced with the truth (right and wrong), was not defensive, and didn't avoid the question. Maybe this is living water? She finally stopped running away from herself and others. The woman saw that Jesus was different and that he was more than a prophet. She concludes,

> *"I know that Messiah" (called Christ) "is coming. When he comes, he will explain everything to us.*
>
> *Then Jesus declared, "I, the one speaking to you—I am he."*

Something amazing happens next: the Samaritan woman left her water jar, went back to her town, and said to the people there, "Come, see a man who told me everything I ever did. Could this be the Messiah? They came out of the town and made their way toward him" (John 4:28–29).

Jesus chose the right therapy strategy. Hours earlier, she was fearful, not wanting to see anyone, and now she is proclaiming about Jesus to her whole town. What an amazing transformation she experienced. She went from living in fear to now living by faith. Jesus did not tell her to go to town; she went of her own volition. A good counselor always lets the client find their own path to wellness. Fear shrinks our world and steals our dreams. This woman found a more significant purpose than her phobia, her gender, her ruined reputation, or social stereotypes. Here's another story of an overcomer who battled his fear to achieve an extraordinary feat:

> A former Royal Marine has a fear of open water and has become the first person to row solo and unsupported from North America to the UK. This 3,000-mile journey was exceptionally dangerous due to the freezing weather and powerful currents. In his solar-powered boat, Dave "Dinger" Bell, 49, sailed from New York to the UK while battling tropical storms, ten-foot waves, and a fear of open water. Bell described being physically sick and trembling while rowing across the ocean before he safely arrived in Newlyn, Cornwall. He spent 119 days at sea alone.
>
> – brightersideofnews.com

Scripture and Emotional Insight

There was a progression of revelation that the Samaritan woman was able to gain about Jesus due to the encounter she had with him. For her, Jesus starts out as a Jew, then a sir, then a prophet, and then the Messiah. When she saw who Jesus really was, she immediately transformed emotionally. In her excitement of meeting the Messiah, she left her jar, even though the reason she came was for physical water. When one has a purpose greater than themselves, it eclipses their personal fears.

Quick Self-Care Tip

Setting small goals to overcome fears is essential when dealing with severe phobias. The woman at the well broke through her fear of people's judgment of her by talking to them about the Messiah. If this is too much, set a smaller goal. Because of her interaction with Jesus she decided to no longer hide but come back into society. Jesus helped her to overcome her fears and regain control of her life that had been greatly out of control. One must constantly monitor their anxiety, step away when it gets too high, and avoid a relapse. The key here is not to succumb to our fears but to excel in our faith.

Chapter 5

Jesus and Grief

The Five Stages of Grief

Grief has been said to have five distinct stages that can fluctuate and change over time. The process is different for each person, so if you support someone going through it, being mindful to practice compassion and patience can be highly beneficial.

- **Denial:** The first stage is called denial, and this is in place to give the individual time to process what has happened and start to recognize that there has been a loss. It allows time to look at what has happened and figure out how to move forward after losing the person.

- **Anger:** Because anger can be a more socially acceptable emotion than admitting to being scared, this can be the next stage that comes up. The biggest problem with anger is that it can push others away, so being mindful of connecting and reaching out to get support can be highly beneficial.

- **Bargaining:** Bargaining is a coping mechanism that individuals might use to find a source to change the circumstances. You might find an individual making promises to change behaviors or do something different to change the outcome of what has happened or what is happening.

- **Depression:** Depression sets in once the reality of the situation hits. It can be problematic because, depending on the level of depression, the individual may feel like being by themselves more, so this is another incredibly important time to have support while processing these feelings.

- **Acceptance:** The last stage is called acceptance, and it essentially means that the pain is not gone but that the individual is accepting what has happened. There can still be sadness present, but there is an understanding that things need to continue even without the person.

– whitepinefunerals.com

Losing someone close to us is never easy, and we all cope differently. I am currently helping a client whose brother passed away suddenly and who has experienced intense grief for the last nine months; it almost cost him his marriage. I have personally seen my share of grief by officiating funerals and giving final prayers to the dying. When we look at Jesus' life, there is a situation of grief that stands out with Mary and Martha's brother Lazarus. We know the story that Jesus raised Lazarus from the dead. I want to focus on the emotional grief in this story. When Martha saw Jesus after her brother died, she confronted him: "Lord, if you had been here, my brother would not have died." Sometimes we want to blame others or God for the passing of our loved one. Mary showed her desperation as she fell at his feet and said, "Lord, if you had been here, my brother would not have died. When Jesus saw Mary weeping, and the Jews who had come along with her also weeping, he was deeply moved in spirit and troubled." Jesus walked into a grief storm, and people were vulnerable. What a great opportunity for him to preach on the realities of heaven and hell, but instead he chose to listen and console. Jesus could have been businesslike, gone to the tomb, and bypassed the emotional drama. He could have put up an emotional boundary and saved himself the pain.

However, Jesus immersed himself in the pain of Mary, Martha, and their friends. His spirit and heart were filled with sorrow, and he wept with them. When the Jews saw his tears, they said, "See how he loved him!" Jesus had the world on his shoulders but showed empathy to two women. To show that mental health care has always been around, Jesus was using person-centered therapy (Carl Rodgers), where "empathy, congruence, and unconditional positive regard" are used. Many who read this have lost loved ones, and at times, we feel we grieve alone. Hopefully, reading this chapter will reassure you that Jesus emotionally connects with your personal pain, and when you weep, he weeps.

Grief Sensitivity (Personal Narrative)

I served as a police chaplain for a couple of years. I was called out to a few 911 incidents in which loved ones had passed away. I remember one situation because the girl was about my son's age. The girl had chronic health issues and died in her sleep. I remember entering their home, and it was hectic and emotional. The mother was wailing, police officers were securing the scene, and CSI was there examining the body for any foul play. My job was to console the family and answer any questions about the process of care for the deceased. I was there about an hour and said maybe ten words, and as I prayed over her body, I was holding back my tears, thinking how I would feel if I went into my son's bedroom in the morning and found him lifeless and cold. Finally, the parents said their goodbyes, and the girl was taken out to the van to go to the morgue. I walked out to the front yard to console the tearful father, and an officer came up to him and said, "I'm sorry for your loss, and at least you have another one," alluding to the fact that they had two children and still had one left! I was absolutely shocked at the insensitivity and did not know what to say to the grieving father. Sometimes one needs to be secure in saying nothing and just being present rather than trying to say something that might be inappropriate and hurtful. Many of us say these things because we don't know what else to say. Remember that everyone processes grief differently, and even the most faithful can question God. Often these statements can come across as insincere and dismissive of their pain. A dear friend of mine, Dr. Dawn Harris, put the following list together. She, unfortunately, passed in 2018. I teach master's level classes in counseling. One of the classes is on grief, and this is an exercise that all my students participate in.

What Not to Say

- I know how you feel. (You don't.)

- I understand. (You have not walked in her shoes.)

- He's better off now. (We can't say this about people we don't know.)

- She's in a better place. (We can't say this about people we don't know.)

- It was his time to go. You are one of the lucky ones.

- Do you have other children?

- It was God's will.

- There was a reason; we just do not understand.

- Everything happens for a reason.

- You need to get on with your life.

- Time heals all wounds. (Loss can stay with you.)

- This too shall pass.

What to Say

- I'm so sorry. (Sometimes even that is too much.)

- There is no way I can understand how this must be for you. How's today?

- What do you need right now?

- Say nothing.

- Just listen attentively. Be there.

- Offer a hug (if appropriate and if invited).

- Pray with them (if appropriate and if invited).

Chapter 6

Jesus and Self-Harming

Self-harm includes behaviors such as:

- Cutting, burning, or hitting oneself
- Binge eating or starvation
- Putting oneself in a risky situation
- Abuse of drugs or alcohol
- Overdosing on prescription medications

Psychosocial signs:

- Lack of interest in hobbies that were once enjoyed
- Disengaging from social interactions
- Having difficulties communicating with loved ones
- Drastic mood swings
- Changes from one's usual eating and sleeping schedule

–healthdirect.gov

Demons! When we think of demons, we think of red creatures with horns and pitchforks. The Bible mentions demons forty-two times, but the word has all but disappeared today from everyday Christian speech. We also exaggerate demonic behavior as the absolute antichrist with foaming at the mouth and climbing up walls. But demonic behavior can just be being prideful! So where have all the demons gone?

> Liberal Christians have long abandoned belief in demons. They consider Bible passages about demons to be of little value. These passages from the Christian Scriptures simply reflect the pre-scientific view of the biblical authors living in Palestine in the 1st and 2nd century C.E.   –religioustolerance.org

In our twenty-first-century church, we have secular words for demonic behavior, like "He has issues," "She needs therapy," and "He needs medication." How can we address the problem when we do not use the biblical words for it or look for a biblical solution? How does the medical field handle demon possession? Many doctors agree that we are emotional, physical, mental, and spiritual beings. However, we live in a day when the physical comes first, mental/emotional is second, and spiritual is most often not even considered. Here's an article on how modern medicine treats those claiming to have demonic fears:

> "Usually, we treat 600 to 700 a month," says Dr. Hardat Sukhdeo, director of Jackson Memorial Hospital's Crisis Intervention Center. "But last month, we had 900 people come for help.... We worked our tails off—maybe there was a strong pull from the moon or something." The belief that demons can infiltrate a person's body is old hat to the Jamaicans, Haitians, Bahamians, Cubans, and Puerto Ricans who live in the Miami area, he said. The patients are given strong tranquilizers to calm them; then staff members try to

soothe away their fears.
–Paul Tan Lee, *Encyclopedia of 7700 Illustrations*

When we downplay demons from the pulpit, in the pews, and in the medical field, if demons do exist, what hope do we have? We must be open to looking at mental health through a spiritual lens as well, according to Dr. N. Anderson:

> We must realize that we are not only physical but also spiritual beings. Therefore, some conditions (mental illness) are psychological, and some are spiritual.   –Dr. Neil Anderson, psychiatrist

Jesus' next intervention involves a man with manic behavior. I want us to have an open mind and not get lost in the demonic language but try to see this story from a psychosocial and compassionate perspective. A man who lived in the tombs was erratic and violent, and his behavior had estranged him from his family. At night he could not sleep, and he cried out. The pain was so immense that many nights he self-harmed by cutting himself with stones. What would you do if this was your friend or a loved one? Call 911 and have them admitted into a psych ward? The locals did not have a modern mental health facility, so they chained him up to calm him down! What is impressive is that this story was written 2,000 years ago and this man had textbook psychosocial symptoms (see above) that made him high risk; today he would be diagnosed with nonsuicidal self-injury (NSSI). Has self-harming disappeared today? No; due to the pandemic, it has become an even worse crisis, especially for the young.

> The most significant spikes were discovered early on in the pandemic, as the overall number of self-harm insurance claims for mental health issues among young people ages 13 to 18 in March and April of 2020, as a percentage of all medical claim procedures, was nearly double compared to the prior year. Specifically, claims related to overdoses among that age group jumped up 119% in April 2020 versus April 2019, while claim reports for generalized anxiety and major depressive disorders rose 94% and 84%, respectively.
>
> –Fair Health data, fairhealth.org

Self-harming is an age-old problem, and thousands of people are suffering every day due to it. I have personally helped many with self-harming tendencies. If in counseling we also use spiritual weapons to help our clients, we could quite possibly be saving a whole generation! First century or twenty-first century, we still have the same struggles and pain. Let us see how Jesus helped this man in distress.

When Jesus approached the demon-possessed man, "he shouted at the top of his voice, 'What do you want with me, Jesus, Son of the Most High God? In God's name don't torture me!' For Jesus had said to him, 'Come out of this man, you impure spirit!'" (Mark 5:7–8). What do we do when our loved ones are loud, using defensive and hurtful speech (you always, you never, I hate you)? It seems like they don't want us around, but many times it's a cry for help. We have to find the courage to stay in there with our loved ones but still maintain healthy boundaries. Take breaks and personally seek help. Timing is everything, and you must choose your moments to have honest, straight talk with your friend or loved one (more instruction in "Therapist Note," below).

With Jesus' help, the demons left the man, and witnesses were amazed when "they saw the man who had been possessed by the legion of demons, sitting there, dressed and in his right mind." Wow! What a transformation—the torment, crying, violent erratic outbursts, and self-harming stopped. The man was so grateful he wanted to go with Jesus, but Jesus told him, "Go home to your own people and tell them how much the Lord has done for you, and how he has had mercy on you." He could have gone home, stayed there, got a job, and lived an everyday life. But no, he took his gratitude and used it in the Decapolis. The Decapolis was a group of ten cities in Syria (two of these cities, which you may know, are Damascus and Philadelphia).

As a result, the man went away and began to speak in the Decapolis about how much Jesus had done for him. Moreover, all the people were amazed. In this chapter, Jesus used humanism therapy, which focused on developing the best in this young man and helping him make the right choices for himself. Jesus did not tell him to be an evangelist, but his healing led him to a greater purpose to help others be demon-free.

Personal Narrative

Self-harming is not only cutting; it can be anything we do to harm ourselves intentionally. I have a self-harming habit of overeating. I have gained forty pounds since my thirties. There are nights when I just don't care and eat with no regard for my health. When I stop caring about myself, the demons are winning, leading to other sins like impurity and laziness, which can lead to depression. It is as if, when there is one demon, the others want to join the party! I must be more mindful of the spiritual battle and put on the whole armor of the Lord to fight these temptations (Ephesians 6:10–11).

Spiritual insight

The Decapolis city of Philadelphia is only mentioned in Revelation 3. A church was established there, but it was not planted by Paul or Peter, nor was it sent out in Acts 2. The only way this church was planted was by the demon-possessed man. Wow! He went from being one who indulged in self-harm to one helping others to be set emotionally and mentally free. Very inspiring!

Therapist Note (Pick Your Moments)

So far, we have seen Jesus use humanistic, reality, CBT, and person-centered therapies! Do you want to know the most effective cognitive therapy strategy of all time? Are you ready? It's listening. Yes, it seems simple but complicated, especially when you are tired and emotional. Jesus won hearts because he listened, and people felt heard. Many of us see little results with our loved ones because they do not feel understood. If someone you love is faced with depression, anxiety, mood swings, and even self-harming behaviors, without empathic connection from others, no progress will be made. It is vital that you offer them support and show them that you care about their well-being, but first, it takes courage to engage. First, listen to them, hear their pain (do not interrupt), do not judge, and do not give pat religious answers. Just listen! Again, being understood is a great anxiety reliever. If those who are in distress begin to feel calmer, you can offer to pray for them, if they are OK with it. DON'T mention demons; that will freak them out! Pray for their comfort and for freedom from their mental and emotional distress (in private, you can pray whatever you want). While the incident is still fresh, you must persuade them to see a professional counselor (Christian or secular) to help continue the conversation about their mental health by checking in with them to see how they are doing. If they are unwilling to seek help, they must understand that when they harm themselves in this way (with self-harming, it could happen several times), everyone who loves them suffers too. Also, it is not fair for you to hold all the emotional weight (explain how it affects you: lack of sleep, dread coming home, etc.). Lovingly say that the next time this happens, you will have to seek help for them and protect your own mental well-being; if you say this calmly and lovingly, they will usually understand. They are giving you permission to get them help. Take it!

If you need support, call Lifeline on 13 11 14. If you think your safety or another person's is at risk, call triple zero (000) or 911 immediately.

–healthlinedirect.gov

Chapter 7

Jesus and S.A.D.

(Spiritual Abuse Disorder)

Psychosocial Symptoms

- General apathy
- Sense of guilt if one misses a meeting
- Sense of mistrust of leaders
- Shallow relationships
- Feeling alone
- More anxiety than faith
- Lack of motivation to be spiritual (read Bible/evangelize)
- Constant sense of judgment/shame/guilt
- People pleasing
- Guarded (reluctant to be open/honest)

If you have any of these symptoms for six months or more, please see a specialist.

In our twenty-first-century society, we love our labels (gender and race), and mental health probably leads the way by creating nearly 300 of them in DSM-5. Back in the '70s, we called people just "crazy" or "not all there." Now we have painstakingly dissected psychosocial behaviors and given them a tag. So, if we are holistic beings—mental, physical, emotional, and spiritual—why don't we have labels for spiritual conditions? Actually, the term "spiritual abuse disorder" does not exist, but why not? It makes total sense. Is it just like the demon situation, present but we just don't address it? Could it be a great deception? If the church is not talking about mental abuse, what about spiritual abuse? If we don't acknowledge a possible problem, we can't address it. Hence this scripture:

> *The Spirit clearly says that in later times some will abandon the faith and follow deceiving spirits and things taught by demons.* (1 Timothy 4:1)

What is spiritual abuse? To those who are spiritually minded, they can see this as the greatest of pains experienced, eclipsing any mental, emotional, or physical hurt they may have endured. This scripture states that we must be spiritually on our guard and have a clear spirit and soul.

> *May God himself, the God of peace, sanctify you through and through. May your whole spirit, soul and body be kept blameless at the coming of our Lord Jesus Christ.* (1 Thessalonians 5:23)

Spirit, soul, and body! How are my soul and spirit doing? How often do I think of my soul? The Bible makes it clear that a prerequisite to getting to heaven is being whole and blameless in my spirit, my soul, and my body. When

I look at this scripture, I realize we are only touching the surface of how deep this hurt can go and what is at stake. One can be alive but spiritually dead inside.

Following this thought, if we are in a weak spiritual community, we can be oblivious to these offenses. We can spiritually bludgeon each other and not know it. Why is spiritual abuse so painful? One reason is that when we come into the church, we assume it to be a safe place, and we trust everyone. We open ourselves up, and we get hurt easily by a senseless word or act. Why does this hurt so much? Because in the world we expect people to be sinners and hurtful, but not in the church. This kind of hurt happens when our guard is down; therefore, we may not have felt this kind of pain since we were but a naive child. This can have a catastrophic impact on one's view of church and leadership. One might think, *Then who can I trust?* One can wonder if anyone is safe. As a result, the person can pull back and become disheartened and apathetic.

Church Business and People Usury

Another factor of deceptive spiritual abuse is a seemingly harmless church calendar. How can a calendar be spiritually harmful? Let me finish! All churches have their specialized ministries, celebrations, and special events. Larger churches may pay people to organize these, but smaller churches use nonstaff people who have full-time jobs and family. Year in and year out, they have the responsibility to put on events, some of which, such as conferences, can take hundreds of hours to plan and execute. It is nice for the first couple of years, but after a while it can become a burden, and then some individuals might dread when the event is coming up on the calendar. They feel trapped because no one else wants to touch it. They are miserable and becoming critical of the 80 percent that "does nothing." This can happen leading small groups, volunteer groups, children's ministry, AV, or worship. There are many ways that serving in the church can become hazardous to one's spiritual health. Ministry staff sometimes are scared to ask their volunteers how they are doing because they might have no one to replace them. I have seen individuals on AV and worship teams have full meltdowns in the sanctuary, and to make matters worse, no one says anything, and it is like nothing has happened! The ministry staff and others just wait for the next meltdown. We cannot use and burn out people for the sake of keeping a calendar! So, what is the answer? Unless there are enough volunteers to handle the event, you simply don't have it. Not enough help in the children's ministry, no children's ministry. If we can't give deacon Smith a break from planning the father-daughter dance, and we can't find a replacement, we won't have one. It sends a message that we look after those who serve (which we don't do enough of). It is unfortunate that many have become victims of these abuses and now don't volunteer for anything. They were using their gifts and it turned into graft (English slang for hard, tireless work).

Mercy Triumphs over Judgment

If the church has young or immature leaders who are

full of zeal, it is possible they can run over people's hurts and not have much empathy. As a young minister, I was harsh and prideful. I look back and pray for forgiveness from God and from those I hurt. Unfortunately, some burned-out leaders become neglectful, not protecting the flock from gossip and not dealing with conflict and sin properly, hence compounding the spiritual abuse.

Speaking the truth without love can be another form of spiritual abuse. Talking to people using a judgmental tone with no mercy is also abusive (James 2:13). These issues can make the church unsafe and cause people to withdraw. Sometimes church sermons can be packed with what we "should do" versus the "why" behind what we should do. Here's an example:

> *Therefore, I urge you, brothers and sisters, in view of God's mercy, to offer your bodies as a living sacrifice, holy and pleasing to God—this is your true and proper worship. Do not conform to the pattern of this world, but be transformed by the renewing of your mind. Then you will be able to test and approve what God's will is—his good, pleasing and perfect will.* (Romans 12:1–2)

When you read this, what stands out to you? Is it being a living sacrifice, not conforming, being transformed, renewing the mind, or focusing on his will and purpose? Preaching these do's week in and week out produces burnout and guilt. We miss the true motivation of "God's mercy." Without this fuel we will grind, and the spiritual abuse may continue. Again, we feel that a workshop, guest speaker, larger conference, or new annual theme will turn the tide, but it does not. The hurt in the pews and frustration from the pulpit continue.

Fragile Leadership

It wasn't your stereotypical depression.
I could get out of bed every day, and I did.
I kept praying and reading my Bible.
But my speed decreased to a snail's pace.
And hope felt like it had died.
My motivation and passion dropped to zero
(make that zero Kelvin).

Many leaders are feeling this way today! With racial tensions, COVID illnesses and deaths, meeting restrictions, secular dominance in media and academia, and general life stressors, ministers are tired. A Barna poll shows that 1500 ministers are leaving each month. This brings up another spiritual disorder: ministry anxiety disorder (M.A.D.), which is not a clinical disorder. Here are some of the symptoms that a church leader might have:

1. Your motivation has faded.

2. Your main emotion is "numbness"—you no longer feel the highs or the lows.

3. People drain you.

4. Little things make you disproportionately angry.

5. You're becoming cynical.

6. Your productivity is dropping.

7. You're self-medicating or in other hidden sin. (Your coping mechanism has gone underground or dark.)

8. You don't laugh anymore.

9. Sleep and time off no longer refuel you.

> –Carey Nieuwhof,
> "9 Signs You're Burning Out in Leadership"

We can be completely oblivious to the needs of our ministers and believe that they are doing fine, but these statistics don't lie:

- 70% of pastors do not have someone they consider to be a close friend.

- 80% of pastors expect conflict within their church.

- 84% of pastors desire to have close fellowship with someone they can trust and confide in.

- 95% of pastors report not praying daily or regularly with their spouse.

- 57% of pastors believe they do not receive a livable wage.

- 78% of pastors report having their vacation and personal time interrupted with ministry duties or expectations.

- 70% of pastors report that they have a lower self-image now than when they first started.

- 66% of churches have no lay counseling support.

- 80% believe pastoral ministry has negatively affected their families.

- Only 1 out of every 10 pastors will retire as a pastor.

–Barna Research

Knowing these stats, why would anyone want to be in the ministry? There can be a significant toll on their finances, family, and faith! The amount of spiritual hurt and disillusionment in the church today is at an all-time high. It reminds me of the quote from Jarrid Wilson I used earlier: Churches present an image of perfection/performance, but "churches should look more like psych wards."

I recently saw a sober video of pastor James Gailliard, in which, instead of preaching, he sat on a chair and shared his heart about his personal burnout. He expresses that "before, there were good days and bad days; now they're just days. I am numb."

He describes the people he has buried, as well as dealing with intense suffering with members he cares for deeply. Ministers can suffer from a type of PTSD. Why is that?

Here is the definition of PTSD: "Post-traumatic stress disorder (PTSD) is a condition that occurs after experiencing or witnessing a traumatic event." Ministers are the first to engage the sick, dying, and suffering in the church. I have seen people take their last breath and consoled many in their grief and suffering. Having several cases a year, as I have had during my twenty-nine years of ministry, can take a toll on a person. Ministers carry an emotional and spiritual weight that many do not understand.

Gailliard describes three types of people in the church: the ones who support the "weight" by giving and serving the ministry; the ones who are the "weight" that genuinely needs help and pastoral care, and the ones who push down the "weight." These individuals do not help, but they are critical and relentlessly push down the weight onto the second type (while nodding and smiling at them!). He states that "these folk come for me" and "beat me up all week." He accepts that all churches have these people, but he said, "I'm not healing quickly enough," and that it is a spiritual issue. He wanted to preach from his "scars and not his wounds" and did not want to spiritually abuse the congregation on a Sunday morning. We must ask ourselves, "Which of these three types am I?" A good indication is encouragement. How often do I go up to my minister and sincerely thank him for his sacrifice (emotional, spiritual, and financial)? Ministers bleed too!

Yes, I have M.A.D., and you have S.A.D.! No one is immune to spiritual abuse and disappointment. We are all in this together, and we must fight this spiritual war arm in arm. We have to put down our pitchforks and pick up compassion and truly express sincere appreciation for each other.

Personal Story

I have been in church as a member for thirty years and as a minister for twenty-nine, and I have witnessed numerous hurtful personal attacks, slander, and even racism. I have been fired from the ministry and not had enough money to pay my bills. To top it all off, I have had my life threatened by other "Christians." I felt anger and have had questions and made accusations like "How can Christians do that or say that?!" and "They don't admit their own fault." I really have to fight for righteousness and pray that bitterness does not set in. So Marvin, how did you keep your faith? Before I was a Christian, I used to physically hurt people, and that has gone through my mind! But I can't do that; I'm a Christian. I have to look to Jesus. He helps me to get a healthy perspective: Jesus was sold and abandoned by "Christians." In many cases I have approached these individuals. In some instances, we have reconciled, and in others, sadly, we have not. I look to Jesus to help me at times when I'm hurting:

> *When they hurled their insults at him, he did not retaliate; when he suffered, he made no threats. Instead, he entrusted himself to him who judges justly.* (1 Peter 2:23)

When I'm really struggling, my wife has interceded

and reminded me that I should probably talk to someone about my vengeful feelings and pray. I am thankful for her concern for my spiritual well-being and for her not letting the spiritual abuse I am feeling develop a bitter root in my heart. Again, Jesus was not immune to hurt and betrayal. He fought to keep his faith, especially dealing with the Pharisees and teachers of the law (who claimed to know God). They constantly attacked his faith and character and eventually plotted his death! Here is a scripture that demonstrates Jesus' struggle:

> *During the days of Jesus' life on earth, he offered up prayers and petitions with fervent cries and tears to the one who could save him from death, and he was heard because of his reverent submission.* (Hebrews 5:7)

We must fight to keep our spirit, soul, and body clear of resentment, bitterness, and revenge, because our eternal destiny is at stake. We have to submit to God's purposes in our life and see that Jesus was purified and glorified through the cross (suffering). We must know when to fight and when to submit.

Scripture Encouragement

"Come to me, all you who are weary and burdened, and I will give you rest. Take my yoke upon you and learn from me, for I am gentle and humble in heart, and you will find rest for your souls. For my yoke is easy and my burden is light" (Matthew 11:28–30). If we learn from Jesus, we will find rest for our minds and souls.

Must-See Video

Pastor James Gailliard's heart-moving sharing: https://fb.watch/bEQOX1FaWr/

Chapter 1–7 Observation:

As we conclude this section of the book, I want the reader to observe that Jesus was a social rights pioneer for the marginalized; he was a lone voice for the outcast (sick/minorities/poor) and especially women (Mary, Martha, the Samaritan, the bleeding woman, and the adulterous woman). Jesus brought compassion and empathy into the world, which rarely existed in the first century.

Part 2

Mental and Emotional Toughness

Chapter 8

Emotional Maturity

(Nurture and Nature)

On a scale of 1-10 (10 being the best) where do you fall on the Emotional Toughness Scale of Emotion

Joy/Appreciation/Empowered/Freedom/Love

Passion

Enthusiasm/Eagerness/Happiness

Positive Expectation/Belief/Optimism

Hopefulness/Contentment

Boredom

Pessimism

Frustration/Irritation/Impatience

Overwhelment

Dissapointment

Doubt

Worry

Blame

Discouragement

Anger/Revenge

Hatred/Rage

Jealousy

Insecurity/Guilt/Unworthiness

Fear/Grief/Despair/Powerlessness

Move UP the emotional scale

The strain on couples and the family is greater than ever, with sales of online self-help divorce agreements rising by 34 percent during the pandemic, and with those seeking counseling services having increased by 1000 percent (WebMD). Ever-growing overhead, work demands, and life responsibilities have us stretched and stressed like never before, and who suffers? The family! The family gets our emotional fumes. If we add in our own emotional baggage and hurts and the lack of self-care, you can see why, as parents, we can be walking around like emotionally numb zombies.

I grew up in the UK in an interracial family in the '60s. Interracial unions were not accepted anywhere. We moved into an all-white neighborhood, and someone put graffiti on our sidewalk saying, "Ni—ers go home." If this were today, Al Sharpton and the press would be there, and public outrage would ensue! Sadly, this was my reality back then; however, we just moved on. We didn't have much choice on where we lived because of Section 8 housing. Growing up in this era, there was no Black Lives Matter or PC culture. People openly expressed their views on race, and one knew where they stood. As a child, people found me to be an easy target to unload their racist venom upon. All through my life, it was a battle to rise above the color of my skin. If I told you just this side of my story, you would look at me as a victim. However, there is nurture (childhood) in every life, and there is nature (my choices) to be considered. Yes, I have been bullied, but I have also been the bully. My childhood and poor choices led me to alcoholism and reckless living. My way of dealing with conflict was to punch people and curse them out. My actions were selective. I could be nice to some and mean to others. I entertained myself by playing with people's emotions; it got so extreme that a girlfriend came after me with a knife! I preyed on the weak, and she was not the last person I emotionally abused. When I first met my wife, I tried to destroy her fledgling faith in God. Looking back, I see how heartless and selfish I was. I genuinely considered myself as the antichrist at that time. My choices and childhood came to a head when I hit my lowest point. I found myself homeless and hopeless. I was emotionally immature and emotionally abusive. Looking at my narrative, what chance did I have raising children? I could limp through life waving my victim card or take personal responsibility for my actions that I could control (more on my transformation story can be found in *Baguette Moments*). As you can see from my formation, nurture has a tremendous impact on our lives.

Parenting

Are we strangers in our own homes? Do we pay the bills? Finance the functions? Bankroll the living but not invest in the little intimacies that accommodate love and care? Are we present in the hearts of our families in ways that create strong emotional bonds? Do we know our families? I mean, know our families? What fuels them, drives them, speaks to them, and heals them? Or do we treat our families as emotional accessories? Are we doting on them when it is convenient for our careers and appearances, but handling them far too roughly and transferring our trauma onto them?   –Solomon Missouri 2022

As parents, we know we should not starve our children or leave them in the cold. But do we see the hidden neglect we might be perpetrating on them when we overlook the emotional development of our children? It is easily done when you come home tired, and your six-year-old daughter wants to show you her drawing and explain it to you. You are not engaged and look at it quickly and say, "Good job, sweetie," then turn on Netflix or go cook. Many would say there's nothing wrong with this exchange, but it is actually a missed opportunity to get into her world and see what emotionally excites her. This drawing was important to her, but not to you as an adult with real responsibilities. Getting into our children's world helps us have an emotional connection with them, and that connection at a young age can last the rest of their lives. My daughter and I had biweekly Saturday dates. These special times began when she was six years old and ended at eighteen when she went off to college. Why start so young? There will be a tradition set before they are teenagers and independence sets in. Many parents try to connect with their kids, but it can be too late when we see the signs of waywardness (bad grades, addictions, wrong crowd, bullying). These times laid the foundation to help my daughter build up her emotional character by having the tough talks, challenging her selfishness, promoting a positive self-image, helping her forgive others, and establishing emotional boundaries. It is essential to push our kids to become more emotionally resilient as parents. Constantly saving or spoiling your child stunts their emotional development. When they grow up, they can't cope with basic life responsibilities and will struggle in relationships (being unfaithful, addictions, anger, and unhealthy people pleasing).

Even now, my daughter is at college, and we can still spend an hour on FaceTime and talk about our lives. We are best friends. She looks at me as a safe place and confidant. This deep emotional connection helps us talk through conflict, misunderstandings, and any serious life challenges that she might be having. Emotional maturity is developed, not quickly acquired. My daughter is not alone; she has parents who are there for her, which gives her a sense of security as she goes out into a brutal world. Those little daily and weekly connections lay the foundation of emotional maturity. My children were fortunate to have parents who saw the importance of that emotional connection. Considering my upbringing, this parenting story should give you some hope.

That's great, Marvin. What do I do if I am emotionally detached from my family/kids? I have helped many clients to reconnect with their families after years of emotional neglect. Families long for love and are more forgiving than you think. Talk to your partner, set a family meeting, and apologize. Then set a weekly time to eat dinner and play games to have fun. With older kids, you will get some kick-back (apathy and sarcasm) because the prior emotional neglect has hurt them. However, they are testing you. Just stay the course and continue trying to deliberately connect with them. You must make each of these times a priority—schedule it and keep it. This time is more important than meeting with any other relative or friend, or any business call or appointment. Clients come and go, but your family does not.

Adult Emotional Maturity

> When children of emotionally immature parents grow up, their core emptiness remains. As a result, they may live a superficially normal adult life. Their loneliness continues into adulthood unwittingly choosing relationships that can't give them enough emotional connection. They may go to school, work, marry, and have kids, but all the while, they are haunted by the core sense of emotional isolation.
>
> –Dr. Lindsey C. Gibson

Gibson continues by explaining how this emotional isolation can turn into destructive habits (addiction, gambling, alcohol, pornography, or even unfaithfulness) to fill this void, which could eventually jeopardize family and livelihood. One of my specialties in my practice is stress management. Unfortunately, many people today are ill-equipped to handle their life stressors. Dr. J. Del Pozo describes our generation in an article titled "Epidemic of Emotional Immaturity: The deadly cost of not growing up." The church is not immune to this epidemic of emotional immaturity. Peter Scazzero states that "spiritual and emotional maturity cannot be separated. It is impossible to be spiritually mature while remaining emotionally immature." Here are some other signs of adult emotional immaturity:

Signs of Emotional Immaturity in Relationships/a Person

- Poor at communicating their feelings
- Does not process issues that negatively impact relationships
- Can't forgive and move forward
- Has difficulty with empathizing with a partner's feelings
- Does not control their temper during a conflict
- Has trouble understanding how their actions contribute to an issue
- Always seeks reassurance
- Gets defensive and blames you and others
- Won't share weaknesses
- Rigid in thoughts and hard to reason with
- Does not seek advice
- Has friendships but no deep ones
- Is easily angered
- Has a negative comment for most things
- Easily hurt and then pulls away
- Avoids conflict
- Has impulsive behavior
- Never apologizes
- Rarely accepts responsibility for their actions

These behaviors can be pervasive in our homes and in marriages, between siblings and coworkers, between bosses and employees, in churches, and in toxic friendships. Anyone living or working with these traits can feel discouraged and fatigued; one can even feel trapped by the emotional abuse. But then, after a while, we see that most of our friends and family are unsafe, and we have to pay $140 an hour to have a stranger (a counselor) listen to us. Good for me, bad for you!

Emotional Maturity in the Church

> Emotional health and spiritual maturity cannot be separated. It is impossible to be spiritually mature while remaining emotionally immature.
>
> –Peter Scazzero

Is the church immune to the emotional immaturity epidemic? According to Ryan Duncan, who wrote an article on "6 Warning Signs of an Emotionally Immature Christian," we have some challenges ahead of us. Before you read the six things, did your anxiety go up? How do you handle something that challenges your faith or your church? We can use a rationalizing filter to refute anything that challenges our personal doctrine, hence there is no change or repentance. Open yourself up to truth, and it will set you emotionally and spiritually free! Listed are six warning signs:

1. Emotionally immature Christians hate change.

2. Emotionally immature Christians need empathy.

3. Emotionally immature Christians are highly sensitive and easily offended.

4. Emotionally immature Christians can become "spiritual narcissists" (slow to listen, quick to speak).

5. Emotionally immature Christians see the world as black and white.

6. Emotionally immature Christians lack self-awareness.

–crosswalk.com

Emotion is essential to being a healthy Christian. Churches struggle to grow if they are not emotionally and culturally aware. Just as the head of a family can hide behind work, the church can hide behind their large buildings, elaborate worship, and service programs. We must ask ourselves, where is the Holy Spirit and love in what we do? Jesus showed extreme emotion from immense joy (the return of the twelve) and heartbreaking grief (Lazarus' death). In everything Jesus did, he was emotionally and spiritually present. Without emotion, there will be no compassion, no forgiveness, no empathy, and absolutely no love. We can serve tirelessly and have significant Bible knowledge, but it means very little without a deep, emotional, agape love.

If I have the gift of prophecy and can fathom all mysteries and all knowledge, and if I have a faith that can move mountains, but do not have love, I am nothing. If I give all I possess to the poor and give over my body to hardship that I may boast, but do not have love, I gain nothing.... And now these three remain: faith, hope and love. But the greatest of these is love. (1 Corinthians 13:2–3, 13)

Step Up to Maturity

This is a plea to return to our support system, intimate partners, [to create] safe soft spaces, but one must acknowledge the disconnectedness and damage that pushed them away to begin with. At times we want to repair but not review. We want accommodation but not accountability. We won't be cured without the work of healing. But before we move toward the possibility of reconciliation, church, let's question the personal brokenness that breaks up our families.

–Solomon Missouri

Our emotional condition can be hidden behind our accomplishments and how we physically provide for our family or how we serve in the church. For men, it is easy to measure ourselves by our work, hobbies, and chores, and we can hide behind these to not engage with our families. I have worked for Fortune 500 companies and seen men stay at work longer to escape the emotional chasm at home where no one seems happy. As men, we might feel that we have been running away for months and have an emotional mountain to climb. However, do not give up—there is hope. How do we grow in our emotional maturity? The first step is to be honest with yourself and be open about your emotional state. Look at the scale at the beginning of this chapter. Most people live between insecurity and being overwhelmed, and between anger and pessimism. Be honest with who you are! If you don't know, ask someone who spends a lot of time with you. We all have bad days, but living in constant anxiety or frustration is no life at all, and what is it doing to your health? A healthy perspective lives between contentment and joy. Contentment is taking the rough with the smooth and finding emotional balance.

Emotionally mature people take responsibility and apologize for their actions. After being honest with yourself, you need to apologize to those around you. Having this out will hold you accountable to change. The next step is to set obtainable emotional goals. Many of us fail with our goal setting because we set too many of them, and we are destined to fail. If I want to work on my angry outbursts, I have to look at my triggers and responses. Imagine getting angry with your son when he doesn't clean his room. Have a family meeting to apologize for your outburst and ask for help. If the kids are old enough, you can ask, "How can you help me be calmer?" Your kids know what sets you off and will probably volunteer themselves to be a part of the solution. This will be better than constant nagging from you. Do not underestimate the power of humility and an apology. I have apologized to my children many times, but showing consistent personal change gives credibility to my words. We have had several resets when I have apologized and set a new course for the family or in my marriage. Remember, practicing calm, humble communication and setting reasonable goals works.

Emotional Boundaries

> You feel responsible for their feelings, and you feel exhausted and apprehensive.
>
> You feel you can't say no.
>
> You feel defeated when you try to solve their problems.
>
> You feel accused of letting them down.
>
> You have overly intense emotional reactions to them—they transfer their feelings to you.
>
> −Dr. L. Gibson

How many of us feel like this, overly responsible for those we love? We have sleepless nights and high-anxiety days. It never seems to end. There are moments when you feel that they might change, but a few days later, you are back on the emotional roller coaster. In this endless cycle, you must establish an emotional boundary.

> Creating healthy boundaries allows you to take care of yourself and restore a sense of well-being. Boundaries help you self-regulate and take ownership

of your own emotional work while allowing others the dignity of doing theirs, should they decide to do so. As the work of emotional maturity returns to its respective owners, wellness has a better chance of emerging.

–Dr. B. Brogaard

A boundary is set for you and for them. You only let the boundary down when there is a complete change in a concerning behavior. The other party (coworker/friend/partner/child) may test boundaries, especially when they are seriously set. A close friend, your child, or your spouse will probably try to manipulate you and make you feel guilty. Here are some words they might use:

- I'm leaving.
- You don't love me.
- I've done this a thousand times and you never had a problem with it; why are you punishing me now?
- I'm taking the kids.
- You let _____ get away with this.
- Now I can't visit you because of these rules (holidays).
- You acted this way when you were younger.
- You call yourself a Christian!
- I'm going to sleep on the couch.
- I want the money you owe me.
- I'm talking to Mom! (parents have to be in agreement)

Mental Toughness

It will take mental toughness to keep the boundaries in place. I repeat, nothing will change unless you hold your ground. It may be tough for a couple of weeks. They may spread rumors and make you feel guilty. They will get other relatives/friends/coworkers to question your actions, but they don't have to live or work with them! After a couple of weeks, it should calm down, and though you may still hear the odd sarcastic remark being made, it's their immaturity talking. If you see improvement after a few weeks, then let the boundaries down in increments. As behavior improves, it could take months for the boundary to be taken down totally. If the emotional abuse begins again, reestablish the boundary. This will require mental toughness on your part to stay the course. Get into the habit of saying no, especially in the first couple of weeks.

Resource

Try an emotional maturity test at https://www.quizony.com/emotional-maturity-quiz (takes 10 minutes).

Chapter 9

Social Media and Mental Health

> A 2019 study of more than 6,500 12- to 15-year-olds in the US found that those who spent more than three hours a day using social media might be at heightened risk for mental health problems. Another 2019 study of more than 12,000 13- to 16-year-olds in England found that using social media more than three times a day predicted poor mental health and well-being in teens.   —Mayo Clinic

When I first moved to the States, there was no social media, international phone calls were too expensive, and the only way to communicate was by a handwritten letter. Jump forward thirty-plus years; we have Facebook, Facetime, and WhatsApp, and they are wonderful ways to keep in touch. There are many positive things about the internet, but a dark side has caused a significant increase in mental health issues, especially in teens since 2009. Our phones have become our addiction! Without our phone, we feel like we are missing a limb or a loved one. With a vibration or ding, some of us can react like Palov's dogs; we can't leave it alone. I have watched *The Social Dilemma* documentary on Netflix. Some supercomputers span city blocks and monitor every click you make; they record what you watch and tailor a unique catalog of content to keep you swiping. Love puppies, and you will see more puppies; love porn, and you will see more porn. If you like liberal politics, guess what you will get and only get! I left the US in 2010 and came back in 2014 (Facebook went from 500 million to 1.5 billion in that time), and the political polarization was at a fever pitch. If we are only receiving one view of the world, you can see how we can be divided. Racial tension was high when we returned; does this have anything to do with social media? We can blame the left or the right, but when you look at data, it's greed for advertising money and a supercomputer feeding our social media addiction. Google, Apple, and Facebook are the wealthiest companies ever to exist. There is nothing new under the sun—this reminds me of a scripture written 2,000 years ago: "They seduce the unstable; they are experts in greed" (2 Peter 2:14). The most unstable section of our society is the young.

User

I must admit that when our children were young (ages one to three years), we put them in their highchairs with a snack and put on *Veggie Tales* to appease them. It gave us a twenty-minute break. Today, I see young children having a full-on tantrum simply to get their parent's smartphone or tablet. I have seen children as young as eight years old wear their parents down to get their own unmonitored smartphone. Last week, I talked to a teacher who told me a shocking story. She spoke about a TikTok video that showed a violent dare called the "choke out challenge." This video had millions of hits. It showed a boy who choked out a friend, who came back to consciousness, and then they laughed about it afterward. A group of eighth graders in her school watched this video, and one of them decided to run up to a random student from behind and choke him. He lost consciousness and hit the floor so hard he landed on his head and was knocked out cold. He regained consciousness but had a severe concussion and missed several weeks of school. He's recovering from the head injury, but he also has PTSD from this violent attack. The boy who did it was suspended for a year for this grievous assault on a fellow student. He was blindly influenced by this video and never considered the consequences.

Today, we have billions around the world enslaved to their phones, oblivious to the polarizing mind manipulation and long-term mental health issues that they might be placing upon themselves. Edward Tufte has a great insight on the internet: "There are only two industries that call their customers users: illegal drugs and software."

A 2015 study found that social comparison and feedback seeking by teens using social media and cellphones were linked with depressive symptoms. In addition, a small 2013 study found that older adolescents who used social media passively, such as by just viewing others' photos, reported declines in life satisfaction.   –Mayo Clinic

We see people sitting together in restaurants, looking at their phones and not talking to each other. The only time they speak is when they are showing a video! Many of us bring our phones to bed, and we hold that device more than we do our spouse.

How many times do we say, "Wait, let me read this post or send this text"? Many of our children and other loved ones will not engage us anymore because we have become second to their phone. Our lives are now relegated to talking or looking at and envying other people's lives. Tristen Harris, who worked as an early designer at Google, is one of the few speaking out. "It's a digital pacifier when we are lonely or depressed." We use the internet as a mindless escape from stress and responsibilities in our lives. When we post, we are conscious of who will like it or not. We love all the positive comments, but one bad emoji or comment can send us into an emotional tailspin (Chamath Palihapitiya).

Palihapitiya, one of Facebook's creators, laments, "We are looking for fake, brittle gratification," longing for likes, emojis, and shallow comments from others. Today, we are fragile people looking for a better life and desperately seeking affirmation, wishing ourselves to be someone else or somewhere else. How fragile can we be? A nineteen-year-old girl in the UK committed suicide because she did not receive enough likes on her selfie she posted (hollywoodunlocked.com)! So, what's the answer?

An older study on the impact of social media on

undergraduate college students showed that the longer they used Facebook, the stronger their belief was that others were happier than they were. But the more time the students spent going out with their friends, the less they felt this way (Mayo Clinic). We have to get back to old-school socializing methods—face-to-face interactions and no-phone zones. We must watch out for any addictive behavior and ruts we can get in. Here is a scripture to help us: "I have the freedom to do anything, but not everything is helpful. I have the freedom to do anything, but I won't be controlled by anything" (1 Corinthians 6:12 CEB).

Ask yourself, can I give up my phone for a day or a week? If something controls or masters you, Jesus is not Lord of your life, because we can't have two masters. Consider how your phone has made you unapproachable and distracted. Ask your kids/spouse if they have felt that way. Then apologize and change. Talk about phone-free times as a family (dinners, dates, game nights, etc.). Affirmation starts at home, not on our phone!

Therapy Note

The audience influenced the most by social media is eight—to—nineteen-year-olds. Take some time to get into their world, see what they are looking at, and talk about it. Please help them to process the content responsibly; otherwise, their peers will be their biggest influence.

Resource

Parents should watch with their teen or preteen The Social Dilemma on Netflix (PG13, some language).

Smartphone Boundaries: https://www.hiboox. com/at-what-age-should-children-get-phone

Chapter 10

Get Your Own

(Jesus and Tough Love)

"At that time the kingdom of heaven will be like ten virgins who took their lamps and went out to meet the bridegroom. Five of them were foolish and five were wise. The foolish ones took their lamps but did not take any oil with them. The wise ones, however, took oil in jars along with their lamps. The bridegroom was a long time in coming, and they all became drowsy and fell asleep.

"At midnight, the cry rang out: 'Here's the bridegroom! Come out to meet him!'

"Then all the virgins woke up and trimmed their lamps. The foolish ones said to the wise, 'Give us some of your oil; our lamps are going out.'

"'No,' they replied, 'there may not be enough for both us and you. Instead, go to those who sell oil and buy some for yourselves.'

"But while they were on their way to buy the oil, the bridegroom arrived. The virgins who were ready went in with him to the wedding banquet. And the door was shut.

"Later the others also came. 'Lord, Lord,' they said, 'open the door for us!'

"But he replied, 'Truly I tell you, I don't know you.'

"Therefore keep watch, because you do not know the day or the hour." (Matthew 25:1–13)

Jesus showed tremendous compassion to the Samaritan woman, the bleeding woman, and Martha. However, this passage sees Jesus differently; he has little to no compassion for five of these virgins. Let's examine the passage and see why.

This Bible parable is about the kingdom of heaven, namely, how to get into heaven. Even as a nonbeliever, I believed in a "better place" after death. Jesus spoke in parables to help us think about our character and its consequences. We can get caught up on virgins and wedding traditions here, but we must look at the moral of the story and the eternal ramifications. There were ten individuals; five were wise, and five were foolish. The wise took extra oil, and the foolish did not. Some were prepared for the call and others were not. When the foolish ones tried to light their lamps, they were out of oil and ordered, "Give us some of your oil; our lamps are going out." Give us or give me! This statement almost sounds like a command, as though they are entitled to or have the right to the oil. They could have said, "Can I have" or "Can you lend me." Also, the words "Give us" sound like toxic groupthink. Just because many people feel a certain way doesn't mean they are right! How many people today want something for nothing? Was this sentiment felt just in Jesus' time, or is it happening now?

Culture of Hypersensitivity

> We are the most coddled generation in history, and it is apparent in both our work ethic and our outlook on life. We expect things to be hand-delivered to us, we love attention and praise for doing what is required of us.... Therefore, our generation has to be one of the most pampered and whiney generations in history. This extends all the way to the manner in which people take criticism. It is impossible to give constructive criticism to people in our generation as we all think that we have the answers to everything.
>
> —elite daily

This is a quote from Eddie Cuffin, a Generation Y individual who also shares this about his generation: "Having a whole generation with sensitivities to correction and even positive criticism keeps them immature emotionally." Even as a therapist, it can be challenging to talk about life's realities with them. Let's get back to the parable: The wise could have felt guilty for not sharing their oil and given in to peer pressure. Instead they replied no, "buy your own" (MSG). These women were shocked that they said "NO" to them.

> "No" is a small word that packs a lot of power. It carries with it an invisible force that can make it feel overly oppressive, or even like a dirty word. We're **often** taught that saying "no" is a negative thing, that it

hurts those around us and causes us to miss out on new, exciting opportunities. It's no wonder so many people are uncomfortable saying it, but the truth is, when you say "no," you're not saying, "I hate you," and you're not insulting someone, you're simply exercising your right to say "no" because it is a right, not a privilege.

–Toni Robbins

The five wise virgins exercised their right to say no. Later the foolish came back with lighted lamps and expected a special concession made for their lack of preparation and to be let in. The host (Jesus) responded, "I do not know you." The wise did not people please and coddle the foolish, and neither did Jesus. People pleasing is prevalent in our society, but how should we view it in the kingdom of God?

Am I now trying to win the approval of human beings, or of God? Or am I trying to please people? If I were still trying to please people, I would not be a servant of Christ. (Galatians 1:10)

What is the difference between the bleeding woman and the five foolish virgins? It is circumstances versus choices. The bleeding woman had no say in her illness, but the virgins could have been ready, and they were not. Jesus has no patience for those who know better. Those who feel that others owe them something and are entitled will be left out of the kingdom of heaven. The word "no" must be used in helping people enter in.

Jesus took everyone on their own merit; we see this with Martha, the bleeding woman, the Samaritan woman, and the ten virgins. Jesus said yes to some and no to others. He used all his love to try to help people to repent. One can't be just a "no person," being harsh and condemning, or a "yes person," being too afraid to tell the truth to others. We cannot reward or keep quiet about bad behavior. We must say no to manipulation, abuse, sin, criminal activity, selfishness, and freeloading. The demon-possessed man was set free by a no. A no can actually save a person! We cannot stay silent, or people please with those close to us (friends/spouses/kids).

We must learn how to say, "No!"

Things to Ponder

- How do I feel about this parable?
- Is it too harsh, or is it justified?
- Have societal norms diluted my convictions?
- How do I feel about the word "no"?
- How often do I say no?
- Is there anyone I should say NO to?
- How do I handle correction?
- Could my mindset compromise my eternal destiny?

Enabling

The wise virgins did not enable the foolish ones. But how can you tell when people are lazy versus just needing help? Here's a scripture that helps me with relationships and counseling:

And we urge you, brothers and sisters, warn those who are idle and disruptive, encourage the disheartened, help the weak, be patient with everyone. (1 Thessalonians 5:14)

First, we must be patient with everyone. Then if we help the weak, they will get strong, and if we encourage the disheartened, they will get courage. So, after helping and encouraging, the only thing left is the idle and rebellious (making a broad categorization here). If they are not showing any eagerness in any area of their life, they are probably sick or depressed. But if they show energy and excitement to go out and play a sport or party with their friends and will not help around the house or go on a date, that is selective behavior pointing to laziness, or it/you may not be a priority! One must speak up or put up a boundary (Chapter 8); otherwise, one can become disheartened and discouraged. We cannot exasperate ourselves with people who don't want to change. These five virgins were idle, and the wise would not tolerate it. The spiritual lesson here is that if you help the idle, they might not appreciate it or change. For people to change, they have to take personal responsibility for their lives and stop blaming others. Here's another scripture that I have found myself using more and more in the church:

Therefore, my dear friends, as you have always obeyed—not only in my presence but now much more in my absence—continue to work out your salvation with fear and trembling. (Philippians 2:12)

Work out your own life! Work out your own relationship! Work out your own finances! Work out your salvation! Churches can be a haven for emotionally and spiritually underdeveloped individuals, especially when one-over-another discipling is involved. We can rely on people asking us, "Did you pray, did you tithe, did you read your Bible or are you in sin?" If we are not careful, we can possibly be propping people up so that they are living by accountability measures rather than by their own reverent fear of God and being Spirit motivated. These people run the risk of remaining perpetually weak, depending on others, and even blaming others when they struggle. It is time to BE WISE and say (with love) "Get your own." We have to empower, not enable.

I want to leave you with a scripture:

> *No discipline seems pleasant at the time, but painful. Later on, however, it produces a harvest of righteousness and peace for those who have been trained by it.* (Hebrews 12:11)

Resources

How to say no: https://www.wikihow.com/Learn-to-Say-No

Tough love: https://www.betterhelp.com/advice/love/what-you-need-to-know-about-tough-love/

Enabling: https://www.healthline.com/health/enabler#how-to-stop

Part 3

Mental Awareness

Chapter 11

Healthy Self-Talk

Many people are conscious of an inner voice that provides a running monologue on their lives throughout the day. This inner voice, or self-talk, combines conscious and unconscious beliefs and biases about ourselves and provides a way for the brain to interpret and process daily experiences. Our self-talk can be cheerful and supportive or negative and self-defeating. Self-talk can be beneficial when it's positive, calming fears and bolstering our confidence

—Psychology Today

Self-talk is something we all do. It is our dialog with ourselves, and unfortunately, most of us, as we get older, have more negative self-talk, especially when we add in past hurts and failures. As a result, we can get down on ourselves and quit before even trying. Why is this?

When you have a negative, fear-based, shameful experience or an insecure thought, your mind wraps around it like Velcro. When you have a positive experience—for example, when you receive a compliment, or somebody affirms and congratulates you, it slides off you like melted butter on a Teflon skillet. Our brains are hardwired to record negative experiences and quickly forget positive experiences. The human mind is attracted to the negative. It's why we get so caught up in gossip. It's why bad news is good for ratings. Humiliation sticks with us for days. Shame and hurt can stick with us for years. But we are not nearly as affected by the positive feedback we receive.

–Dr. Rick Henson

Negativity sticks like Velcro! Our natural human state is fear based, and without being mentally intentional, life can turn bleak. If we don't fight these thoughts, we will succumb to a miserable, faithless existence or be filled with anxiety. We pooh-pooh anyone's good ideas and put a dark cloud over other people's dreams. Some of us are unconsciously there; this can include me occasionally, because my wife has to stop me raining on people's success or good news; she calls me Mr. Neg-Fest! (Is that in DSM-5?) This reminds me of a '70s song that depicts how many feel: "The Logical Song" by Supertramp, which recalls how life is wonderful and seemingly beautiful and magical when we are young, but then we are taught to be "sensible, logical, responsible, practical" and are shown a world where we can be "dependable, clinical, intellectual, cynical."

Childlike Mind

What happened to our childhood spirit of being opportunistic and fun loving? Where did it go? Somewhere in our journey of life, we lost our positive outlook. Some of this comes from childhood trauma, life hurts and disappointments, or just taking life too seriously. I wrote a whole book on this called *Capes and Tiaras: The Power of Childlikeness* (IPI). In the book, I wrote about the benefits of having a childlike heart. I strive to maintain a fun-loving, light, and positive spirit. So, what do self-image and self-talk have to do with our spiritual state?

> *Do everything without grumbling or arguing, so that you may become blameless and pure, "children of God without fault in a warped and crooked generation."* (Philippians 2:14–15)

According to this scripture, we are children of God, and it is possible to keep a pure and blameless heart and mind in a crooked and depraved world. Wow! When do we stop being a child of God? The answer is "Never!" So I'm a child of God, but my mind can sometimes be that of a grumpy, anxious old man. There is a significant disconnect here!

If I'm a child, what type of child am I? Am I a baby, toddler, preteen, or teen? How does God see me?

If I am still in need of God, trust is the key. The smaller the child, the more the trust. Teens are independent and think they know better, but a toddler is continually in need. Accepting our childlike status will help us surrender to God's will. This needy state will help us not want to control things as much, and we will experience less anxiety and stress. Yes, less anxiety and stress! When I say child-likeness, I don't mean childishness. I'm talking about keeping the creative, lighthearted, fun-loving, short memory of a child. The key is keeping this disposition throughout the course of our lives.

> Adults whom we call geniuses are those who somehow retain and build upon that childlike capacity throughout their lives. —Dr. Peter Gray, psychologist

Healthy Self-Image

How do we keep this childlike capacity and regain that sense of wonder and awe of God? It starts by destroying the unhealthy negative self-images that often lead to having a warped perspective of God.

> *Praise be to the God and Father of our Lord Jesus Christ, who has blessed us in the heavenly realms with every spiritual blessing in Christ. For he chose us in him before the creation of the world to be holy and blameless in his sight. In love, he predestined us for adoption to son-ship through Jesus Christ, in accordance with his pleasure and will—to the praise of his glorious grace, which he has freely given us in the One he loves.... You were marked in him with a seal, the promised Holy Spirit, who is a de-posit guaranteeing our inheritance until the redemption of those who are God's possession—to the praise of his glory.* (Ephesians 1:3–6, 13–14)

This passage is about our image in Christ. By being a child of God, you are chosen, unique, treasured, loved, and have sonship/daughtership in Christ with a full inheritance. You are rich. You were not given the leftovers but instead, every spiritual blessing that heaven has to give! This truth was hard for me to believe when I was growing up in Section 8 housing and when I was temporarily homeless. I must remind myself of my heavenly Father's vision and promises. A healthy perspective of who we are will help us erase the false self-image that Satan wants us to believe. Yet another one of Satan's deceptions!

Mind Change

> For years, research has shown that, over time, our experiences literally reshape our brains and can change our nervous systems, for better or worse. Now, neuroscientists and psychologists like Dr. Hanson are zeroing in on how we can take advantage of this "plasticity" of the brain to cultivate and sustain positive emotions.
>
> —Michael Bergeisen, greatergood.com

Here is some good news: Plasticity beats Velcro! So yes, our brains can rewire themselves to be more positive. To reshape our brain, we must be intentional in what influences it. Ask yourself, who or what makes me mad or anxious, or is unhealthy for me mentally? In biblical terms, this plasticity is called repentance and transformation of the mind. Again science is simply catching up with what God already knows. Spirituality will help erase the negative tapes.

Here's a scripture that states that we are not held captive to our negative self-talk:

> *The weapons we fight with are not the weapons of the world. On the contrary, they have divine power to demolish strongholds. We demolish arguments and every pretension that sets itself up against the knowledge of God, and we take captive every thought to make it obedient to Christ.* (2 Corinthians 10:4–5)

There are many cognitive strategies for overcoming negative self-talk when we use God's tools. We now have access to divine power to fight our mental battles. God wants to set us free from the mental bondage of negativity and anxiety so that we can be a child of his again.

Be Honest

The first step to turning back the clock is good self-talk. But good doesn't mean painless; we have to be honest with ourselves about our shortcomings and take responsibility for our choices. Some of us act like a victim when our decisions put us in a predicament. Example: We can't pay the rent, but we just bought a new car. Then we whine that we don't have any money and expect others to pay. Another one is we're overwhelmed at work, but we're the one who accepted the promotion. Maybe the job is too much for us, but we stick it out in our pride while our family suffers around us.

The same outcome can happen when starting a business or going back to school. Every action has a reaction. When people are on their deathbed, they usually don't lament over not opening another business or working more. Instead, they regret not having spent more time with their loved ones.

This honest self-talk will stop the victim mindset and start you on a productive one. The second step is the humility to acknowledge your selfishness and apologize to those around you. Step three is reprioritizing your life. It might mean getting a new job or cutting back hours, or selling the new car; all these are painful but liberating. These decisions can possibly help free you up to spend better time with your family and God. Step four is consistency. All this will free you up to prioritize what is most important (God, family, and self-care). The anxiety will go down, and the childlikeness within you will return.

Humble yourselves, therefore, under God's mighty hand, that he may lift you up in due time. Cast all your anxiety on him because he cares for you. (1 Peter 5:6–8)

As a little child, we need God's mighty hand for protection because we are vulnerable and weak. So we need to look up (have a faithful mind) and reach out in need (be humble), and he will lift us up! God cares for you, so don't be fearful (anxious).

10 Spiritual Truths about Me! (Read this when you are feeling less than yourself.)

Finally, brothers and sisters, whatever is true, whatever is noble, whatever is right, whatever is pure, whatever is lovely, whatever is admirable—if anything is excellent or praiseworthy—think about such things. (Philippians 4:8)

- I am a new creation.
- I am reconciled with God.
- I am no longer a slave to sin.
- I am forgiven of my sins.
- I am washed, sanctified, and justified.
- I am transformed into his likeness, and I am perfect.
- I have the mind of Christ.
- I am chosen.
- I am at peace with God.
- I am loved, I am loved, I am LOVED!

Resources

Self-talk https://www.psychologytoday.com/us/basics/self-talk

Who we are in Christ: https://www.compellingtruth.org/who-in-Christ.html

Chapter 12

Glory in Weakness

Individualism is the moral stance, political philosophy, ideology, or social outlook that emphasizes the moral worth of the individual. Individualists promote the exercise of one's goals and desires and so value independence and self-reliance and advocate that the interests of the individual should achieve precedence over the state or a social group.   —slife.org

America built its culture on individualism and strength. The words of self-empowerment in the quote mentioned above are: one's goals, desires, self-reliance, independence, and that an individual has precedence over the group. The American mantra is to be strong and independent. I lived in Texas for several years, and it prides itself on being called the Lone Star State. In its constitution, they have the right to separate from the union and become their own country!

When I was younger, I looked at emotion as a weakness and mocked people who showed it. I enforced my point of view by manipulating and strong-arming weak people. This quote reminds me of my younger self.

A man's spirit is free, but his pride binds him with chains of suffocation in a prison of his own insecurities.
—Jeremy Aldana

In the past, my pride and insecurities suffocated me to the point of being homeless and becoming an alcoholic. Even today, I have a hard time being "weak." I'm still too slow to apologize and very rarely cry. As I've grown older, I see that it takes emotional courage to express weakness and emotions. How often do you apologize or rationally express your real feelings? Many of us express emotion, but it comes out in anger, and we can use extremely hurtful speech, which is destructive. This comes back to growing in our emotional and spiritual maturity. Jesus naturally expresses his full range of emotions, from sincere joy to immense pain. Our emotional vulnerability reflects our spiritual maturity. Paul understood this principle:

> If I must boast, I will boast of the things that show my weakness. The God and Father of the Lord Jesus, who is to be praised forever, knows that I am not lying. (2 Corinthians 11:30–31)

This scripture goes against the American DNA. We are conditioned to boast about our strengths. When we meet people socially, we state our job, position, and education. It is the social norm to brag about our accomplishments. Those who show constant strength send a message that they need no one. Those who are always complaining are draining. Yet this scripture states that no one is immune to the storms of life:

> *"He causes his sun to rise on the evil and the good and sends rain on the righteous and the unrighteous."* (Matthew 5:45)

Everyone has days of sunshine and days of rain. But it's not sunny all the time, and rain clouds will eventually pass by. Life has good days and bad. We all know this, but somehow, we forget and get shocked by the "rain of life" when it comes. Somehow, we feel as though if we share our "rainy days," we will be rejected. But when we are open, a fantastic thing happens:

I am struck by how sharing our weakness and difficulties is more nourishing to others than sharing our qualities and successes. —Jean Vanier

This is true. People are drawn to authentic, honest people. At conferences, my wife shares about her childhood abuse. Afterward, she has a line of total strangers, some in tears, sharing about their own abuse with her. Openness breeds openness. There is a reverse power to weakness. Everything inside us tells us not to show it (our pride), but when we do, that's when the magic happens. Paul had his rainy days, and he surrendered to them:

> *He said to me, "My grace is sufficient for you, for my*
> *power is made perfect in weakness." Therefore I will boast*
> *all the more gladly about my weaknesses, so that Christ's*
> *power may rest on me. That is why, for Christ's sake, I*
> *delight in weaknesses, in insults, in hardships, in persecu-*
> *tions, in difficulties. For when I am weak, then I am strong.*
> (2 Corinthians 12:9–10)

Paul danced in the rain. He must be from the UK (it rains a lot). As he embraced his weaknesses, he got stronger. There is a power in bringing our insecurities to the surface. Satan can't use them against us. There is nothing hidden, so nothing can be exploited. No one can say anything that you haven't divulged. This makes you authentic and approachable to deeper relationships. What does science say about openness and the mental and physical benefits of it? Here's some research on the matter:

> Openness is correlated with higher measures of
> well-being, including overall happiness. People high in
> this trait feel more positive and have warm and loving
> relationships with the people around them. Research
> has not found any noteworthy correlation between
> openness and anxiety or other mood disorders.
> —*Psychology Today*

People who are open about their weaknesses have less anxiety, a clear conscience, more faith, and deeper relationships. Expressing weaknesses makes us stronger and happier.

Here is a list to help us differentiate between being weak and expressing weakness:

Weakness that shows strength	Weak character hidden in pride
• Humility	• Easily quits
• Vulnerability	• Is half-hearted
• Openness	• Avoids conflict
• Confession	• Is defensive
• Seeks advice	• Blames others
• Quick to apologize	• Exhibits anger/rage
• Accepts responsibility	• Is manipulative

Personal Challenge

Here's a little test: Try being open with a weakness (bad habit, mistake you made, embarrassing moment) and see what happens. Show your spouse/child some humility and see how shocked they are. Apologize to a friend and see what their response is. Be strong!

Part 4

Spiritual and Mental Self-Care

Chapter 13

Mindfulness

Many of us are guilty of going through the motions of day-to-day life while failing to invest any real concentrated effort into any of it. We drive from place to place, often not remembering how we got there because we are tuned out, lost in our heads, distracted with technology, and suffering from mental fatigue. We finish the workday exhausted while feeling we've accomplished nothing of any real value. We participate in conversations and fail to remember more than a quarter of it. Our distraction is eroding our relationships, time management abilities, success, and productivity. Our society is overlooking what is important and failing to honor what matters most. We sacrifice time with our families and friends to answer emails and messages. We give up necessary sleep to check alerts and texts.   —Neen James

I have lost count of how often my wife reminds me where we are going because I'm in the wrong lane to go to our appointment. I go on autopilot. I am mindless and lost in my head thinking about something else or nothing at all.

The lights are on, but no one is home!

Practicing mindfulness seems to be a twenty-first-century phenomenon that has swept the States, but mindfulness has been around for centuries.

> Definition of mindfulness: A technique in which one focuses one's full attention only on the present. The state or quality of being mindful or aware of something. —dictionary.com

Mindfulness means being present, being aware, and being conscious. Practicing it in its simplest form is listening to your spouse or kid and focusing on the task at hand without your mind wandering. In addition, mindfulness can help to relieve stress and anxiety.

> Strengthening the mind is not done by making it move around as is done to strengthen the body, but by bringing the mind to a halt, bringing it to rest.
> —Ajahn Chah

It is coming to a halt and being still! Being still and sitting in silence scares a lot of people because it brings our guilt, shame, and failures to the surface. Here's a "shocking" study:

> It was not how hard people found the challenge but how far they would go to avoid it that left researchers gobsmacked. The task? To sit in a chair and

do nothing but think. So unbearable did some find it that they took up the safe but alarming opportunity to give themselves mild electric shocks in an attempt to break the tedium. Two-thirds of men pressed a button to deliver a painful jolt during a 15-minute spell of solitude. One man—an outlier—found thinking so disagreeable he opted for a shock 190 times.

—The Guardian

Wow! Meditation seems so easy, but it can be torture if we are not at peace with ourselves. Is it possible to change ourselves without slowing down? According to Peter Scazzero, we must shed our "false self" to live authentically in our new "true self"—powerful spiritual breakthroughs take place when we slow down. So, what is our false self? This is where our failures, negative self-image, negative self-talk, shame, guilt, and insecurities lie. If we have the courage to face our weaknesses and inner demons, we will find our "true self."

Jesus and Mindfulness

What does Jesus say about mindfulness?

"Look at the birds of the air; they do not sow or reap or store away in barns, and yet your heavenly Father feeds them. Are you not much more valuable than they? Can any one of you, by worrying, add a single hour to your life?

"And why do you worry about clothes? See how the flowers of the field grow. They do not labor or spin. Yet

I tell you that not even Solomon in all his splendor was dressed like one of these. If that is how God clothes the grass of the field, which is here today and tomorrow is thrown into the fire, will he not much more clothe you—you of little faith?... Therefore do not worry about tomorrow, for tomorrow will worry about itself. Each day has enough trouble of its own." (Matthew 6:26–30, 34)

Just imagine it's a beautiful day in Jerusalem; you are outside on a mountainside in the shade under a tree. There's a nice breeze, the grass is thick and comfortable (no bugs), and the people around are friendly. This new teacher is preaching a radical message about loving your enemies and having treasure in heaven. Then he says, "Look at the birds of the air." You look up in the tree and see sparrows chirping and fluttering from branch to branch. They are not stressed. Then he tells you to focus on the flowers. Right beside you is a sunflower. You intently see details you've never seen before: the seeds, the clumps of pollen, the bee sucking the nectar, and the bright yellow of the petals. Then he talks about the grass in the field. You touch the grass around you; it is cool to the touch and very lush. You realize that your stress and worry have gone because you are present and taking in what is around you. In this passage, Jesus practices several mindfulness strategies.

- **Pay attention.** It's hard to slow down and notice things in a busy world. Try to take the time to experience your environment with all your senses—touch, sound, sight, smell, and taste. For example, when you eat a favorite food, take the time to smell, taste, and truly enjoy it. —Mayo Clinic

- **Accept yourself.** Treat yourself the way you would treat a good friend. —Mayo Clinic

- **Live in the moment.** Try to intentionally bring an open, accepting, and discerning attention to everything you do. Find joy in simple pleasures. —Mayo Clinic

- **Everyday exploration.** The art of mindfulness is about making the mundane fascinating. The more you tune in to your senses, the more everyday objects can take on new meaning and new life. —thejoywithin.org

Jesus makes it clear that he wants us to live in the now by saying, "Therefore do not worry about tomorrow, for tomorrow will worry about itself." Jesus wants us to be present, not carrying past failures or feeling overwhelmed and fearful about tomorrow. Jesus rebukes us because it takes faith to live in the now and not be anxious.

> Few of us ever live in the present. We are forever anticipating what is to come or remembering what has gone. —Louis L'Amour

It is impossible to change our ways when we are not present; it is hard to learn and truly participate in life when we are in this state of mind. A psalmist wrote this 3000 years ago: "Be still, and know that I am God." Can I truly know God unless I am still? David was a man in touch with his emotions, and he expressed them fully in his writings. He wrote many psalms about meditating on God's word, laws, precepts, blessings, and creation. To have a deep emotional relationship with God, we must slow down and meditate daily on his glory, power, and blessing. It starts with being still. If you will recall, there is hope because the mind has plasticity, and we can repent.

> There are two types of seeds in the mind: those that create anger, fear, frustration, jealousy, and hatred and those that create love, compassion, equanimity, and joy. Spirituality is germination and sprouting of the second group and transforming the first group.
>
> —Amit Ray

Start with baby steps: look at a clock with a second hand, start with a minute of being still, and add a minute a day; or use one of the resources below. If you can get to twenty minutes, your brain will reset (headspace.com). By doing this, you will produce serotonin, which will calm you.

The 24/7 Counselor

Suppose I told you that I would waive my hourly rate, and I can be on call 24/7. Most people would say, "Yes, please." As a Christian, you have a counselor at your beck and call: "When the Counselor has come, whom I will send to you from the Father, the Spirit of truth, who proceeds from the Father, he will testify about me" (John 15:26 WEB).

The Holy Spirit guides you and even directs you as to what to say. We have the holy hookup! Prayer is another way to focus and be still. Prayer fills our minds with heavenly things and thankfulness. Prayer lets us get out our anxiety and stress by being open with our Father in heaven. These are all God's tools for mental wellness. Stillness, meditation, prayer, and the Holy Spirit are all mindfulness tools. Again, there is nothing new under the sun!

Other Meditation Exercises with Scripture

Focus on your breathing. When you have negative thoughts, try to sit down, take a deep breath, and close your eyes. Focus on your breath as it moves in and out of your body. Sitting and breathing for even just a minute can help. —Mayo Clinic (Psalm 150:6)

Sitting meditation. Sit comfortably with your back straight, feet flat on the floor, and hands in your lap. Breathing through your nose, focus on your breath moving in and out of your body. If physical sensations or thoughts interrupt your meditation, note the experience and then return your focus to your breath. —Mayo Clinic (Psalm 48:9)

Body scan meditation. Lie on your back with your legs extended and arms at your sides, palms facing up. Focus your attention slowly and deliberately on each part of your body, in order, from toe to head or head to toe. Be aware of any sensations, emotions, or thoughts associated with each part of your body. —Mayo Clinic (1 Corinthians 6:19)

Walking meditation. Find a quiet place ten to twenty feet in length, and begin to walk slowly. Focus on the experience of walking, being aware of the sensations of standing, and the subtle movements that keep your balance. When you reach the end of your path, turn and continue walking, maintaining awareness of your sensations. —Mayo Clinic (Proverbs 3:17)

Purposeful Waiting: For those who feel they never have enough time, waiting on others can be quite frustrating. Waiting for someone or something is actually a great opportunity to sit in stillness and monitor all around you. Maybe you are waiting for a zoom call to start; use this opportunity to look around and explore as though it was your first time being in the room. Maybe you are waiting in a coffee shop; use this opportunity to listen to the sounds of the people and the cups clinking. In every moment of waiting lies an opportunity to notice your surroundings with all your senses. —stress.org (Psalm 130:5)

Resources:

7 Christian Mindfulness Exercises: https://www.calminggrace.com/christian-mindfulness-exercises/
12 Fun Mindfulness Exercises: https://www.

stress.org/12-fun-mindfulness-exercises

Quick meditation at work: https://www.the-guided-meditation-site.com/mindfulness-exercises.html

A guide for 20 minutes of meditation: https://www.headspace.com/meditation/20-minute-meditation

Spiritual meditation and devotional book: *Emotionally Healthy Spirituality Day by Day: A 40-Day Journey with the Daily Office* by Peter Scazzero.

Chapter 14

Holistic Care

Sleep

When it comes to mental health, it's essential to look at your total health. Let's start by looking at something as simple as sleep!

If sleep deprivation continues long enough, you could start to hallucinate—seeing or hearing things that aren't really there. A lack of sleep can also trigger mania in people who have bipolar mood disorder. Other psychological risks include:

- impulsive behavior
- anxiety
- depression
- paranoia
- suicidal thoughts
  —healthline.com

People deprived of sleep can have serious mental health issues that could be misdiagnosed.

Food that Helps Mental Health

Increase serotonin: For mood, sleep, pain, and craving control, combine tryptophan-containing foods, such as eggs, turkey, seafood, chickpeas, nuts, and seeds (building blocks for serotonin) with healthy carbohydrates, such as sweet potatoes and quinoa, to elicit a short-term insulin response that drives tryptophan into the brain. Dark chocolate also increases serotonin (foodmatters.com).

Increase dopamine: For focus and motivation, consume theanine from green tea, lentils, fish, lamb, chicken, turkey, beef, eggs, nuts, and seeds (pumpkin and sesame), high protein veggies (such as broccoli and spinach), and protein powders (foodmatters.com).

Antioxidants and magnesium-rich food help anxiety.

Maca is good food for depression.

Supplements: St. John's wort, zinc, magnesium, vitamin D, and omega-3 fatty acids will help your mood and overall mental health.

Increase Your Happy Chemicals

Serotonin: A mood-enhancing chemical in the brain that produces feelings of calmness and happiness. Low levels of serotonin have been linked to depression and anxiety.

Oxytocin: Releasing this neuropeptide promotes social bonding among family and significant others. Oxytocin has also been shown to increase cooperation and teamwork.

Dopamine: This chemical is involved in pleasure and reward. By laughing, the release of dopamine also helps with feeling less anxious. Watch a funny movie.

Endorphins: Endorphins help promote positive feelings and relaxation—they're the same chemicals that cause a runner's high. Through an endorphin-mediated opioid effect, laughter may help ease physical pain.   —insider.com

Prayer and Meditation

Prayer and meditation release serotonin. Doing well spiritually will help your mental health. This will help mood swings, anxiety, and depression. Prayer also taps into divine intervention.

Physical Exercise

Exercise is a natural and effective antianxiety treatment. It relieves tension and stress, boosts physical and mental energy, and enhances well-being through the release of endorphins.

As one example, a recent study done by the Harvard T.H. Chan School of Public Health showed that running for fifteen minutes a day or walking for an hour reduces the risk of major depression by 26 percent.

Evidence suggests that by really focusing on your body and how it feels as you exercise, you can help your nervous system become "unstuck" and begin to move out of the immobilization stress response that characterizes PTSD or trauma.   —helpguide.org

Counseling

Counseling is another tool to help your cognition. Therapy helps unload guilt and change our negative self-image.

Medication

Prayer, meditation, counsel, exercise, and diet can help your mental health. I would make sure you have exhausted these options before considering medication, although I am not against people taking medication.

Free Mental Health Evaluations

Free Depression Test
https://screening.mhanational.org/screening-tools/depression/

Free Anxiety Test
http://www.mydesertview.org/wp-content/uploads/2017/11/BeckAnxietyInventory-Ages-14.pdf

Free Stress Questionnaire
http://www.hcei.org/uploads/5/2/4/3/52438643/stress-questionnaire.pdf

Free Suicide Ideation Resource

https://www.helpguide.org/articles/suicide-prevention/are-you-feeling-suicidal.htm

If you or your child are suicidal or a danger to others, call 911 or 1-800-273-TALK (8255) immediately.

Also, go to mklcounseling.com for couples/stress/anxiety and anger evaluations.

Chapter 15

Keep Your Fork!

Therefore we do not lose heart. Though outwardly, we are wasting away, yet inwardly we are being renewed day by day. For our light and momentary troubles are achieving for us an eternal glory that far outweighs them all. So we fix our eyes not on what is seen, but on what is unseen, since what is seen is temporary, but what is unseen is eternal. (2 Corinthians 4:16–18)

Thank goodness that when we go through hard life challenges, we can rest assured that there must be something better than this! When I reflect upon my childhood, my homelessness, the racism, and ongoing life struggles that I endured, I am grateful for that very truth. Every now and then, I say, "Lord, take me now. I am tired, and I can't do this anymore." I will share my family's ministry journey with you over the last twenty-nine years of my life:

Our calling for the ministry happened when I was twenty-seven years old. I gave up a Fortune 500 job to go into the ministry in Los Angeles. We would have been fired in our first year of ministry because of my pride; however, God came through, and a church in Houston picked us up, so we sold everything and moved. Later we moved to Boston for six years, and both of us were laid off on the same day with two kids, one with autism and a newborn. I cried in a park and put our ministry dreams in his hands. So we sold everything again and moved to Texas. There we served a church for eight years. I got burned out by doing the same pragmatic ministry and put my resignation in, and we had nowhere to go! So again, I put my plans in God's capable hands. God directed us to start a self-funded church in my hometown of Norwich, UK. We sold everything again and moved 5,000 miles with no jobs or place to live. I led the mission team of four and started a private counseling practice (story in Capes and Tiaras). This was the first time my kids lived abroad, and my daughter cried for four months missing her friends. There were times when we didn't have money for rent, but miraculously, a few days before it was due, a donation was made to cover it. In our four years there, we never had a set income to cover our monthly bills, but God provided. God blessed our sacrifice, and many souls were won. When it was time to come back to the States, we sold everything again and arrived in the USA with a few boxes. I wish I could say that this move was easy and that the church experience was pleasant, but this was one of the most painful ministry jobs in my life, with constant divisiveness, gossip, and slander. Through every storm, there are always blessings: we met some lifelong friends, and our kids came to faith. But after six years of constant "weight" it came to a head. I remember one evening when my wife was struggling with her depression. Looking at her tears and the ongoing conflict in the church, I was done! I called a brother and worked out a plan to move to their city and somehow keep my practice. I was fifty-five years old! What was God doing? God, was this it after twenty-eight years of ministry? I have sold everything for you several times and moved six times in six years. We have no retirement, no money in the bank, and now this! I was broken and broke. I had to wrestle on my knees to not become bitter toward God.

So, what did we do next? We sold everything again during a pandemic and moved to Guam! Yes, Guam is 8,000 miles away. I can't explain it. Yet when I thought I was done, somehow God gave us a second wind and we set off to help a small church in the Pacific Ocean that had been without leaders for a few years. Amazingly, God also allowed me to continue my private practice. It's been challenging, but during the pandemic, several souls were saved! Hopefully, our story inspires you that light can come out of the darkness, so don't let go of your "fork."

During those dark times, I held onto hope and the promise of heaven:

> *"They will be his people, and God himself will be with them and be their God. 'He will wipe every tear from their eyes. There will be no more death' or mourning or crying or pain, for the old order of things has passed away."* (Revelation 21:3–4)

What helps me is to know that this struggle will end, and there will be no more pain, mourning, or tears in heaven. I have witnessed plenty of pain in my personal life; and being a counselor, I have seen my share of suffering and heartache in others. So I ask myself why life is so hard. It must mean that heaven will be absolutely amazing! Here is an inspiring story of keeping the hope of heaven alive:

Keep Your Fork

There was a young woman who had been diagnosed with a terminal illness and had been given three months to live. As she was getting her things in order, she contacted her pastor and had him come to her house to discuss certain aspects of her final wishes.

She told him which songs she wanted sung at the service, which scriptures she would like read, and which outfit she wanted to be buried in. Everything was in order, and the pastor was preparing to leave when the young woman suddenly remembered something very important to her.

"There's one more thing," she said excitedly.

"What's that?" came the pastor's reply.

"This is very important," the young woman continued. "I want to be buried with a fork in my right hand."

The pastor stood looking at the young woman, not knowing quite what to say.

"That surprises you, doesn't it?" the young woman asked.

"Well, to be honest, I'm puzzled by the request,"

said the pastor.

The young woman explained. "My grandmother once told me this story, and from that time on, I have always tried to pass along its message to those I love and those who are in need of encouragement. In all my years of attending socials and dinners, I always remember that when the dishes of the main course were being cleared, someone would inevitably lean over and say, 'Keep your fork.' It was my favorite part because I knew that something better was coming... like velvety chocolate cake or deep-dish apple pie. Something wonderful, and with substance!

"So I just want people to see me there in that casket with a fork in my hand and I want them to wonder, "What's with the fork?" Then I want you to tell them: "Keep your fork...the best is yet to come."

The pastor's eyes welled up with tears of joy as he hugged the young woman goodbye. He knew this would be one of the last times he would see her before her death. But he also knew that the young woman had a better grasp of heaven than he did. She had a better grasp of what heaven would be like than many people twice her age, with twice as much experience and knowledge. She knew that something better was coming.

At the funeral, people were walking by the young woman's casket, and they saw the cloak she was wearing and the fork placed in her right hand. Over and over, the pastor heard the question, "What's with the fork?" And over and over he smiled.

During his message, the pastor told the people of the conversation he had with the young woman shortly before she died. He also told them about the fork and about what it symbolized to her. He told the people how he could not stop thinking about the fork and told them that they probably would not be able to stop thinking about it either.

He was right. So the next time you reach down for your fork, let it remind you, ever so gently, that the best is yet to come.

—Roger William Thomas,
A 3rd Serving of Chicken Soup for the Soul

Spiritual Maturity

Cresenda
Jones

God's Will for
Emotional Health
and Healing

Available at www.ipibooks.com

Spiritual Transformation

Transformation

Emotional Intelligence and Freedom

Cresenda Jones

Available at www.ipibooks.com

A Handbook for Christians
Facing Emotional Challenges

Rejoice
Always

Revised and Expanded Second Edition

Dr. Michael Shapiro & Dr. Mary Shapiro

Available at www.ipibooks.com

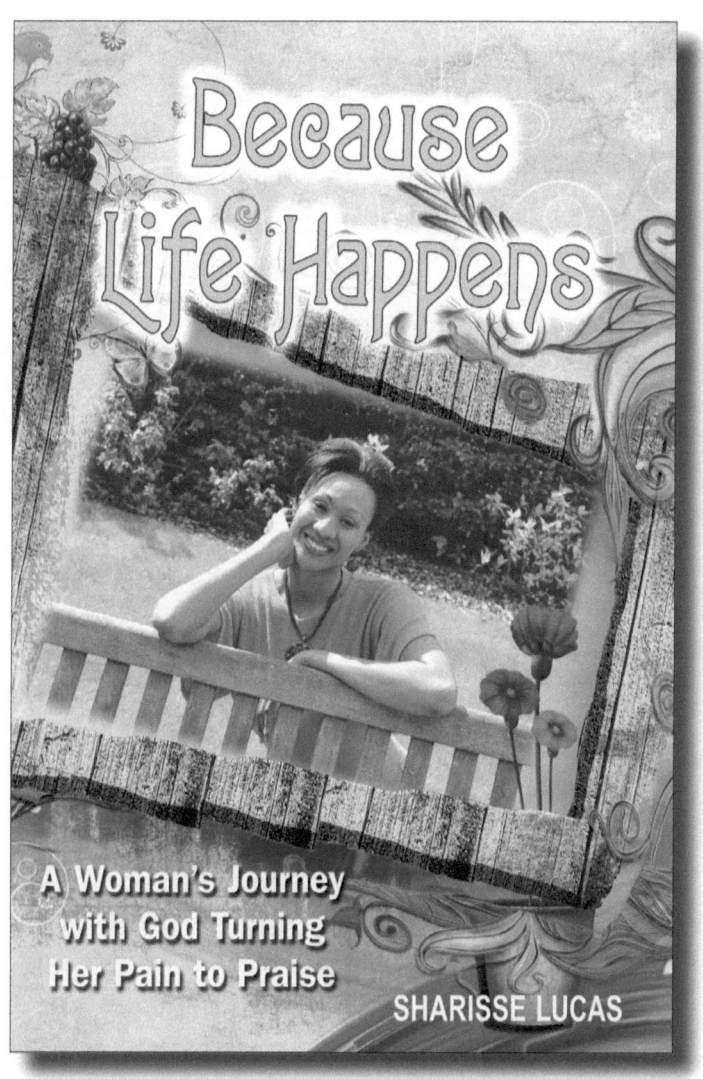

Because Life Happens

A Woman's Journey
with God Turning
Her Pain to Praise

SHARISSE LUCAS

Available at www.ipibooks.com

Marvin K. Lucas

Baguette Moments

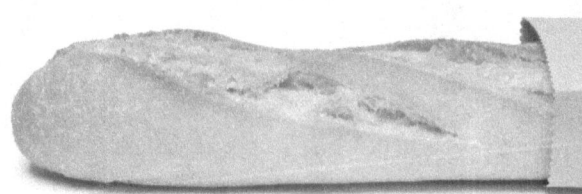

Learning the Power
of Entrustment

Available at www.ipibooks.com

Capes
&
Tiaras

The power of childlikeness

Marvin K. Lucas

Available at www.ipibooks.com

www.ipibooks.com

www.ingramcontent.com/pod-product-compliance
Lightning Source LLC
Chambersburg PA
CBHW021647120626
46545CB00002B/734